READY TO WRITE

A FIRST COMPOSITION TEXT

THIRD EDITION

KAREN BLANCHARD • CHRISTINE ROOT

PEARSON

Longman

We dedicate this book to Owen Baker Root, the newest member of our team.

Ready to Write 1: A First Composition Text
Third Edition

This book was previously published as *Get Ready to Write: A First Composition Text, Second Edition.*

Pearson Education, 10 Bank Street, White Plains, NY 10606

Acknowledgments: We are grateful to Jeff Diluglio, John Dumicich, Carolyn Graham, Jane Sloan, and Robby Steinberg for helping us keep the purpose of this text in focus. We also appreciate the hard work of Donna Schaffer, Gina DiLillo, and Stacey Hunter. Finally, thanks to Pietro Alongi and Paula Van Ells at Pearson Longman for their steadfast support.
Reviewers: Marta Dmytrenko-Ahrabian, Wayne State University, Detroit, MI; Sally Gearhart, Santa Rosa Junior College, Santa Rosa, CA; Lois Hollander, Howard Community College, Columbia, MD; Laura Leek, Sacramento City College, Sacramento, CA; Maisah Robinson, Westwood College, Atlanta, GA
Staff credits: The people who made up the *Ready to Write* team, representing editorial, production, design, and manufacturing, are Pietro Alongi, Gina DiLillo, Christopher Leonowicz, Amy McCormick, Edith Pullman, Carlos Rountree, Massimo Rubini, Barbara Sabella, Donna Schaffer, Jennifer Stem, Jane Townsend, and Paula Van Ells.
Text composition: TSI Graphics
Text font: 10.5 Frutiger Light
Illustrations: Gary Torrisi, except pp. 33, 42, 48, 49, 56, 84 (bottom row), 131 by Susan Detrich and Tom Sperling
Technical art: Tinge Design Studio
Photo credits: Cover, Shutterstock; Pages 8, 10, Superstock; 38, © Royalty-Free/Corbis; 46, © 1999 Randy Glasbergen; 53, 58, Shutterstock; 62, © 2003 Randy Glasbergen; 68, Shutterstock; 83, Courtesy of Christine Root; 89, Shutterstock; 104, © Charles C. Ebbets/Bettmann/Corbis; 111, © Getty Images/Justin Sullivan; 117, Shutterstock; 118, Courtesy of NASA; 120, Associated Press/Jennifer Graylock; 122, Shutterstock; 124 (top), Associated Press/Dario Lopez-Mills, (bottom), Associated Press/Ed Landrock; 128, Shutterstock; 137, © Randy Fairs/Corbis
Text credits: *Singing, Chanting, Telling Tales: Arts in the Language Classroom* by Carolyn Graham, source for "Using Poetry to Write about Memories" and memory poem format on page 126. Reprinted with the permission of Carolyn Graham.

Library of Congress Cataloging-in-Publication Data
Blanchard, Karen Lourie
  [Get ready to write]
  Ready to write 1 : a first composition text / Karen Blanchard, Christine Root.—3rd ed.
    p. cm.
  Previously published as: Get Ready to Write: A First Composition Text, 2nd ed.
  ISBN-13: 978-0-13-136330-4 (pbk.)
  ISBN-10: 0-13-136330-1 (pbk.)
  1. English language—Textbooks for foreign speakers. 2. English language—Rhetoric—Problems, exercises, etc.
3. Report writing—Problems, exercises, etc. I. Root, Christine Baker. II. Title. III. Title: Ready to write one.
  PE1128.B5865 2010
  428.0076—dc22

            2009035733

ISBN-13: 978-0-13-136330-4
ISBN-10: 0-13-136330-1

PEARSON LONGMAN ON THE **WEB**

Pearsonlongman.com offers online resources for teachers and students. Access our Companion Websites, our online catalog, and our local offices around the world.

Visit us at **pearsonlongman.com**.

Printed in the United States of America
9 10—V011—13

CONTENTS

SCOPE AND SEQUENCE

CHAPTER	GRAMMAR GUIDE	PARAGRAPH POINTER	SAMPLE WRITING TOPICS/ACTIVITIES	REAL-LIFE WRITING
1 WRITING ABOUT YOURSELF	• Simple Sentences: Subject, Verb, Object, Complement • Capital Letters	• Paragraph form	• Using the writing process to write a paragraph about yourself and another about a classmate	• Filling out a form with student information
2 WRITING ABOUT YOUR FAMILY AND FRIENDS	• Pronouns: Subject and Object • Possessive Adjectives • Conjunctions: *and*, *but*	• Writing titles	• Using the writing process to write a paragraph about your family, a relative, and a friend • Writing a paragraph about your future family	• Writing e-mails with requests and apologies
3 WRITING ABOUT YOUR ACTIVITIES	• Simple Present: Forming the Simple Present and Negatives	• Paragraph structure	• Using the writing process to write paragraphs about free-time activities and ways to stay healthy	• Writing e-mails about activities

CHAPTER	GRAMMAR GUIDE	PARAGRAPH POINTER	SAMPLE WRITING TOPICS/ACTIVITIES	REAL-LIFE WRITING
4 **GIVING INSTRUCTIONS**	• Count Nouns and Noncount Nouns • Imperative Sentences	• Signal words	• Writing a paragraph about how to make a yogurt milkshake, remove an ink stain from clothing, stop a nosebleed, and carve a pumpkin • Using the writing process to write a paragraph about how to make or do something	• Writing a recipe card
5 **WRITING ABOUT YOUR DAY**	• Prepositions of Time • Frequency Adverbs • Using *before* and *after*	• Paragraph unity • Time order	• Writing a paragraph about someone's typical day • Using the writing process to write paragraphs about a typical weekday and a holiday	• Writing a message on a card
6 **WRITING DESCRIPTIONS**	• Present Progressive • Adjectives	• Using examples • Using details	• Using the writing process to write descriptive paragraphs about yourself; a friend, relative, neighbor, classmate, or teacher; a country's product; the best or worst gift you've ever received; and your dream car or one you like or own	• Filling out an order form • Writing lost-and-found messages

CHAPTER	GRAMMAR GUIDE	PARAGRAPH POINTER	SAMPLE WRITING TOPICS/ACTIVITIES	REAL-LIFE WRITING
7 **WRITING ABOUT PLACES**	• *There is/There are* • Prepositions of Place	• Space order	• Using the writing process to write descriptive paragraphs and/or letters about places: your classroom, favorite room, home, and community; a famous photograph; and a new apartment • Writing personal letters	• Addressing an envelope
8 **WRITING A NARRATIVE**	• Simple Past	• Narrative paragraphs	• Using the writing process to write a narrative paragraph about a personal experience and another based on a photograph of a traffic jam • Using the writing process to write an autobiographical paragraph and several biographical paragraphs • Writing poetry about special memories	• Writing a postcard
9 **EXPRESSING YOUR OPINION**	• Using *should*	• Order of importance	• Using the writing process to write opinion paragraphs about an issue, advice for learning English, and the invention with the greatest impact on society • Writing letters asking for and giving advice	• Writing a letter to the editor

INTRODUCTION

Ready to Write 1 is a beginning-level writing skills textbook for students of English as a Second Language who have some limited knowledge of both written and spoken English. *Ready to Write 1* is designed to acquaint students with the basic skills required for good writing and to help them become comfortable, confident, and independent writers in English.

Approach

Although it is a writing text, *Ready to Write 1* integrates reading, speaking, and listening skills with prewriting, writing, and revising. As in *Ready to Write 2* and *Ready to Write 3*, students are called upon to write frequently and on a broad range of topics. *Ready to Write 1* is based on the premise that students at this level can and want to express themselves in English. What they need in order to do so effectively is an ever-expanding vocabulary base and successive opportunities to write short, confidence-building pieces.

It is our intention in *Ready to Write 1* to introduce, without being overly didactic, the basic skills required for good writing in English. Through an abundance of pair and group activities as well as individual writing tasks, students learn the fundamental principles of the writing process: prewriting, planning, drafting, revising, and editing as they move from sentence-level writing to guided paragraphs and beyond. We believe that having students write early and often instills in them the confidence necessary for successful writing.

The Third Edition

The third edition of *Ready to Write 1* includes these important features:
- additional model paragraphs
- guided practice in the stages of paragraph writing
- targeted grammar practice
- sentence skills practice
- more paragraph pointers
- additional suggestions for further writing practice
- updated real-life writing activities
- appendices with models for using printed and cursive letters of the English alphabet; a list of common irregular verbs; and punctuation rules

Popular features from previous editions have been expanded and appear regularly in this new edition. *You Be the Editor* focuses on the specific grammar point studied in each chapter. *Word Banks* have been enlarged to supply students with additional useful, pertinent vocabulary. *On Your Own* and *Use Your Imagination* provide students with further, less structured writing practice. Students are encouraged to assemble a portfolio of their work comprising the paragraphs, letters, poems, and drawings that they produce throughout the course.

We hope that you and your students enjoy the activities in this text as they get *ready to write.*
—*KLB and CBR*

WRITING ABOUT YOURSELF

INTRODUCING YOURSELF

Learning to write in a new language is not always easy, but it can be fun. If you are learning to speak and read in a new language, you are ready to begin writing, too. The exercises in this book will help you become a better writer in English.

The easiest way to begin writing is to write about things you know well. That often means writing about yourself.

As you complete the exercises in *Ready to Write 1*, you will do a lot of writing about yourself and your life. You might find it interesting and helpful to keep your writing in a special folder called a portfolio.

Make a Cover for Your Portfolio

A. **Look at the cover that a student designed for his portfolio.**

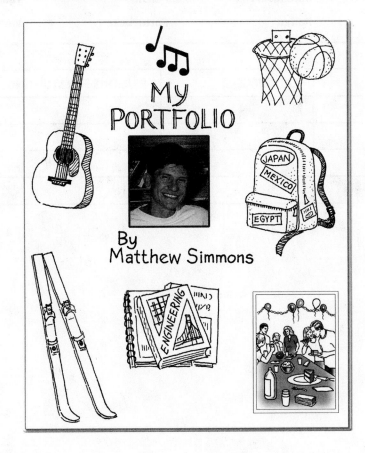

B. Design the cover for your portfolio on a separate piece of paper. Use drawings, photos, and words to describe who you are. Here are some suggestions for things to include:
- your family and friends
- your interests and favorite activities
- sports you like to play or watch
- your job, profession, or major in school
- your favorite places, foods, holidays, activities

C. Share the cover of your portfolio with your classmates.

D. Write your name on the board and teach your classmates how to pronounce it. Does your name have a special meaning in your language? What does it mean?

E. Work in small groups. Tell the people in your group what language(s) you speak. Use the word bank to help you with spelling. Also tell your group why you are studying English. Then complete the chart with the correct information.

LANGUAGES WORD BANK			
Arabic	German	Japanese	Romanian
Cantonese	Greek	Korean	Russian
Czech	Hebrew	Mandarin	Spanish
Dutch	Indonesian	Polish	Thai
French	Italian	Portuguese	Vietnamese

NAME	LANGUAGE(S)	REASONS FOR STUDYING ENGLISH

GRAMMAR GUIDE: SIMPLE SENTENCES

An English sentence is a group of words that communicates a complete thought. Sentences start with a capital letter and end with a period (.), question mark (?), or exclamation point (!). Sentences may be long or short, but all sentences must have a subject and a verb. Many sentences have an object or a complement, too. The order of words in a sentence is important. The most common order for English sentences is subject + verb + object (or complement).

A. **Study the chart below to learn about the parts of a simple sentence.**

PART OF SENTENCE	EXAMPLES
SUBJECT The subject is a person or thing that does the action. It is usually a noun or a pronoun. The subject comes at the beginning of a sentence before the verb.	SUBJECT **Anna** speaks Russian. SUBJECT **He** plays soccer.
VERB The verb usually describes the action. It comes after the subject. The verb may be one word or more than one word.	VERB Marsha **drove** the car. VERB She **is singing** a song.
OBJECT Most verbs (such as *play, read, give, speak*) describe an action. The object is the person or thing that receives the action. The object usually answers the question *What?* or *Who(m)?*	OBJECT Steve opened **the window**. OBJECT My mother is baking **a cake**.
COMPLEMENT Some verbs, called linking verbs, do not describe an action. A linking verb connects the subject of the sentence to information about the subject. The most common linking verb in English is *be*. In sentences with linking verbs, the verb is followed by an adjective or noun, called a complement, which describes something about the subject of a sentence.	SUBJECT LINKING VERB COMPLEMENT Izumi was **tired**. SUBJECT LINKING VERB COMPLEMENT Paulo is **a teacher**.

B. **Circle the verb in each sentence. Underline the subject. Draw a box around the object or complement.**

1. Mr. Robertson is tired.

2. Chris kicked the soccer ball.

3. She is shy.

4. Andrea and Marshall ride bikes.

5. He is a banker.

6. We are watching a movie.

7. They are funny.

8. Leo wrote a paragraph.

9. Mr. Yang is painting a picture.

10. I bought a hat.

C. We use the verb *be* to answer the question "What do you do?" Read the sentences. They all use the verb *be*. Circle the verb in each sentence.

1. I am a teacher.

2. You are a student.

3. She is an engineer.

4. He is an actor.

5. We are salespeople.

6. They are painters.

D. Look at the sentences in Exercise C and answer the questions.

1. Which subject uses *am*? _____

2. Which subjects use *is*? _____

3. Which subjects use *are*? _____

E. Study the word bank. Then find out what some of your classmates do. Ask, "What do you do?" Write five sentences with the verb *be*.

JOBS WORD BANK		
administrative assistant	florist	photographer
artist	hairstylist	plumber
baker	homemaker	police officer
bank teller	journalist/reporter	professor
bus/taxi driver	judge	receptionist
businessperson	lawyer	salesperson
cook/chef	mail carrier	student
dentist	mechanic	teacher
doctor	nurse	veterinarian
electrician	painter	waiter
firefighter	pharmacist	

　　Rose is a receptionist.

1. _____
2. _____
3. _____
4. _____
5. _____

F **Choose four of your classmates. Write two to three sentences about their jobs.**

Example:

Classmate's name: _Rose_____

1. _She works in a doctor's office._
2. _She answers the phone._
3. _She makes appointments._

Classmate's name: _____

1. _____
2. _____
3. _____

Classmate's name: _____

1. _____
2. _____
3. _____

Classmate's name: _____

1. _____
2. _____
3. _____

Classmate's name: _____

1. _____
2. _____
3. _____

GRAMMAR GUIDE: CAPITAL LETTERS

The first word of every sentence begins with a capital letter. Other important words in English begin with a capital letter, too.

A. **Study the rules below for using capital letters.**

RULES: ALWAYS CAPITALIZE . . .	EXAMPLES
1. the first word of a sentence	What is his name? His name is Matthew Simmons.
2. the pronoun **I**	Harris and I like to play tennis together.
3. the names and titles of people	He has a meeting with Dr. Carol Wolf. Let's call Song Yee.
4. the names of streets, cities, states, countries, and continents	The library is on Juniper Street. She is from Austin, Texas. They live in Lima, Peru. Peru is in South America.
5. days of the week and months of the year	His birthday is next Thursday. We're going on vacation in June.
6. the names of languages and nationalities	He speaks Vietnamese. My grandparents are Mexican.

B. **Rewrite each sentence. Add the capital letters.**

1. i like to travel.

   _____

2. yumi lives in tokyo, japan.

   _____

3. when did they get back from mexico?

   _____

4. mr. kim has a meeting on friday.

   _____

5. ali is studying spanish and english this semester.

   _____

6. my birthday is in july.

_____

7. what do you want to do on sunday?

_____

8. let's meet julio for lunch on wednesday.

_____

9. did you see mrs. kara in the library?

_____

WHAT IS A PARAGRAPH?

Most English writing is organized into paragraphs. You will write many paragraphs in this book. A paragraph is a group of sentences about one main idea. This main idea is called the _topic_.

PARAGRAPH POINTER: Paragraph Form

English paragraphs are written in a special form. Follow these rules when you write a paragraph:

1. Indent the first line of each new paragraph about 1 inch (2.54 centimeters) from the margin.

2. Begin each sentence with a capital letter.

3. End each sentence with correct punctuation (a period, a question mark, or an exclamation point).

4. Do not start each sentence on a new line.

_A._ **Read the following paragraph. It is written in the correct form.**

INDENT FIRST LINE
CAPITAL LETTER   PERIOD   BEGINNING OF NEXT SENTENCE

My name is Matthew Simmons. I am from Boston, Massachusetts. I am twenty-one years old. I speak English and a little Spanish. I am an engineering student at Boston University. I love all kinds of sports. My favorite sports are basketball and skiing. I also like to travel, play guitar, and go to parties with my friends.

B. Look at the paragraph. Talk with a partner about what is wrong with it.

my name is Ellen Lang

I am twenty-eight years old

I am from Atlanta, Georgia

my native language is English

I am a chef.

I work at a restaurant called Noodles.

of course, I like to cook.

I also like to play the piano and go out with my friends.

C. Write the paragraph in the correct form.

_____

_____

_____

_____

_____

THE WRITING PROCESS

Most people cannot write a perfect paragraph on the first try. Writing a good paragraph is a process that includes several steps. The three main steps are prewriting, writing, and revising. The exercises in this book will help you practice the steps.

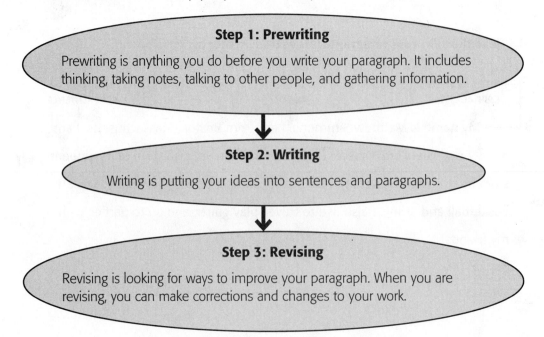

Step 1: Prewriting

Prewriting is anything you do before you write your paragraph. It includes thinking, taking notes, talking to other people, and gathering information.

Step 2: Writing

Writing is putting your ideas into sentences and paragraphs.

Step 3: Revising

Revising is looking for ways to improve your paragraph. When you are revising, you can make corrections and changes to your work.

WRITING A PARAGRAPH ABOUT YOURSELF

Prewriting

Look at the cover of your portfolio again. Think about the words and pictures you included. They will help you get ready to write about yourself.

Writing

A. **Answer these questions about yourself in complete sentences.**

1. What is your complete name?

    _____

2. Where are you from?

    _____

3. Where do you live now?

    _____

4. What language(s) do you speak?

    _____

5. What do you do? (For example, are you a student? Are you a businessperson? Are you a teacher? Homemaker? Lawyer? Bus driver?)

    _____

6. What do you like to do in your free time? (For example, do you like to go to the movies? Do you like to read magazines? Do you like to listen to music? Do you like to go shopping?)

    _____

7. What else do you like to do?

    _____

B. **Use the sentences you wrote to complete a paragraph about yourself. Be sure to follow the rules of paragraph writing.**

My name is _____

_____

_____

_____

_____

Revising

A. Exchange paragraphs with a partner. Read the paragraph your partner wrote. Then use the Revising Checklist to help your partner improve his or her paragraph.

REVISING CHECKLIST	YES	NO
1. Is the first word of the paragraph indented?		
2. Does each sentence begin with a capital letter?		
3. Does each sentence end with the correct punctuation?		
4. Does each new sentence begin next to the one before it?		

B. Use your partner's suggestions and your own ideas to revise your paragraph on a separate piece of paper. Give it the title "About Me" and put it in your portfolio.

WRITING ABOUT A CLASSMATE

Prewriting

A. Work with a partner. Ask and answer these questions. Take notes about your partner's answers.

1. What is your name?

    _____

2. Are you married or single?

    _____

3. Where are you from?

    _____

4. What is your native language? _____

5. What do you do? (Are you a student? Teacher? Lawyer? Musician?)

    _____

6. What do you like to do in your free time? _____

B. What else would you like to know about your partner? Write two more questions to ask your partner.

1. _____

2. _____

Writing

A. Use the answers to write complete sentences about your classmate.

Example:

My classmate's name is Oscar Alvarez.

1. _____
2. _____
3. _____
4. _____
5. _____
6. _____
7. _____
8. _____

B. Use your sentences to write a paragraph about your classmate. Remember to follow the rules of paragraph writing.

My classmate's name is _____

_____

_____

_____

_____

_____

Revising

A. Exchange paragraphs with a partner. Read the paragraph your partner wrote. Make sure the information about you is correct. Then use the Revising Checklist to help your partner improve his or her paragraph.

REVISING CHECKLIST	YES	NO
1. Is the first word of the paragraph indented?		
2. Does each sentence begin with a capital letter?		
3. Does each sentence end with a period?		
4. Does each new sentence begin next to the one before it?		
5. Are all of the sentences your partner wrote about you correct?		

B. Use your partner's suggestions to revise your paragraph on a separate piece of paper. Give it the title "My Classmate" and put it in your portfolio.

ON YOUR OWN

Choose one of the following topics. When you are done with your first draft, revise and edit your paragraph to improve it.

- Write a paragraph about your teacher or another one of your classmates. Use the Prewriting questions on page 10 to help you get started.
- Write a paragraph about someone else at your school or workplace.
- Talk to one of your neighbors or roommates. Write a paragraph about him or her.
- Think of someone you like or admire, such as a movie star, sports hero, or politician. Look on the Internet for information that will help you write a paragraph about that person.

YOU BE THE EDITOR

The paragraph "A Lucky and Happy Man" has eight mistakes with capital letters. With a partner, find and correct the mistakes.

A Lucky and Happy Man

My name is Stanley stoico. I am ninety years old. I am from italy. I moved to San Diego, california, with my family when I was nine years old. I speak italian and english. in my younger years, I had many different jobs. I worked hard and saved my money. In 1965, I started my own business. the business was successful, and i retired in 1993. I like to travel and play golf. I have seen and done a lot in my long life. I am a lucky and happy man.

Filling Out a Form

Fill out the form below with information about yourself.

STUDENT INFORMATION FORM

Please print.

1. Name: _____

                       Last   First   Middle

2. Address: _____

               _____

3. Phone Number: _____

4. E-mail: _____

5. Gender: _____ M   _____ F   Birthdate: _____ / _____ / _____

                                                 MONTH   DAY   YEAR

6. Marital Status: _____ Single   _____ Married   _____ Divorced   _____ Widowed

7. Nationality: _____

8. First Language: _____

9. Other Languages: _____

10. How long have you studied English?

    _____ Never

    _____ Less than 1 year

    _____ 1–2 years

    _____ More than 2 years

11. Do you work?   _____ Yes   _____ No

12. If yes, where? _____ What hours? _____

13. Signature: _____

WRITING ABOUT YOUR FAMILY AND FRIENDS

WRITING ABOUT FAMILY

A. Look at Matthew Simmons's family tree. Then ask and answer the questions with a partner. Use words from the word bank on the next page to help you.

Fred Simmons Harriet Simmons

Stuart Rubin Tammy Rubin

Martina Geller Simmons Alan Simmons

Sam Simmons Evelyn Rubin Simmons

Connie Rubin Berger Steve Berger

Don Strait Beth Simmons Strait Matthew Simmons Greg Simmons

Chris Simmons Melissa Simmons

Owen Strait

Andrea Berger Edward Berger

1. Who are Matthew's parents? _____

2. Who are Matthew's uncles? _____

3. Who are Matthew's aunts? _____

4. Who is Matthew's brother? _____

5. Who are Matthew's cousins? _____

6. Who are Matthew's grandmothers? _____

7. Who is Matthew's nephew? _____

FAMILY WORD BANK

aunt	granddaughter	nephew	son
brother	grandfather	niece	stepfather
child/children	grandmother	parents	stepsister
cousin	grandson	relative	uncle
daughter	husband	sibling	wife
father	mother	sister	

B. Complete the chart with words from the word bank.

MALE	FEMALE	MALE OR FEMALE
uncle		

C. On a separate piece of paper, draw your own family tree. Give it the title "My Family Tree" and put it in your portfolio.

D. Now read the paragraph Matthew Simmons wrote about his family.

My Family

I have a big family, and we all get along very well. My parents' names are Sam and Evelyn. My mother is a teacher, and my father is an engineer. I have one younger brother. His name is Greg. He is seventeen years old. I also have an older sister named Beth. She is twenty-eight years old, and she works at a bank. She is married to Don Strait. They have a baby boy named Owen. I also have four cousins who live in Boston. My mother's parents live in San Diego, but my father's parents live in Boston. They both love to invite the whole family to their house for dinner. Whenever my family gets together, we have a great time.

PARAGRAPH POINTER: Titles

Many paragraphs have a title. A title of a paragraph tells the main idea in a few words. Here are some things to remember when you write titles:

- Titles are not complete sentences.
- Always capitalize the first and last words of a title.
- Capitalize all other important words. Do not capitalize articles (*a*, *an*, *the*) or prepositions (*to*, *from*, *at*, etc.).
- Do not use a period at the end of a title. Do not use quotation marks (" ") around the title. But you may use a question mark (?) or an exclamation point (!).
- Center a title.

Correct the titles.

1. my Favorite hobby _____

2. OUR NEW NEIGHBOR. _____

3. "Free-time is Fun-time" _____

4. Spending Time With Friends _____

5. Fun In The Sun. _____

GRAMMAR GUIDE: PRONOUNS

Pronouns are helpful in writing. They help you connect sentences without repeating the same nouns. A pronoun is a word that replaces a noun. Two of the most common kinds of pronouns are subject pronouns and object pronouns.

Subject Pronouns

Subject pronouns (such as *we*, *she*, *they*) can be the subject of a sentence.

A. Study the chart below. Notice that pronouns can be singular or plural.

SINGULAR SUBJECT PRONOUNS	EXAMPLES	PLURAL SUBJECT PRONOUNS	EXAMPLES
I	**I** speak Arabic and English.	we	**We** have a new house.
you	**You** have beautiful eyes.	you	**You** are my best friend.
he, she, it	SUBJECT *Debbie* is my sister. **She** is eighteen years old. (She = Debbie) SUBJECT *Abdullah* is my cousin. **He** works at a bank. (He = Abdullah)	they	**They** need a new car.

B. **Complete the second sentence in each pair with a subject pronoun.**

1. Mrs. Petty is a teacher. _____ teaches English.

2. My car is green. _____ is new.

3. John and I are brothers. _____ are both students.

4. Steve and Chuck are cousins. _____ live in Taiwan.

5. Jorge loves sports. _____ plays basketball, soccer, and golf.

Object Pronouns

Object pronouns replace nouns as the object of a verb. They usually come after the verb in a sentence.

A. **Study the chart below.**

SINGULAR OBJECT PRONOUNS	EXAMPLES	PLURAL OBJECT PRONOUNS	EXAMPLES
me	Alice loves **me**.	us	Jason drove **us** to the airport.
you	Janet helped **you**.	you	She sent **you** a package.
him, her, it	Fern called *Mrs. Klein*. **OBJECT** Fern called **her**. (her = Mrs. Klein)	them	David e-mailed *Stan* and *Joey*. **OBJECT** David e-mailed **them**. (them = Stan and Joey)

Object pronouns can also come after prepositions, such as *with*, *at*, *on*, *in*, *for*, and *from*.

Examples:

Lenny sang *with* **me**.

I mailed a package *to* **him**.

B. **Complete the second sentence in each pair with an object pronoun.**

1. I e-mailed Mr. Smith. I invited _____ to dinner.

2. I drove my daughter to the train station. I gave _____ money for the train ticket.

3. Pam thinks about her boyfriend. She misses _____ very much.

4. I bought a new car. I drove _____ to school today.

5. I hadn't heard from Ann and Paul for a while. So, I called _____ last night.

6. Teresa always remembers my birthday. This year she gave _____ a beautiful scarf that she made herself.

7. Dave doesn't have a car. I drive _____ to work every day.

C. **Complete the paragraph with the correct subject or object pronoun.**

I love to look at my grandparents' photograph album. _____ (It/Them)
1.
is my favorite thing in their house. I really like the pictures of my mother when

_____ (she/her) was a little girl. _____ (She/Her) looks
2.   3.
so cute with her curly hair and big smile. I also like looking at all of the different cars

my grandfather bought over the years. He loved _____ (they/them),
4.
and he took very good care of each one. My favorite pictures are the ones of my

parents' wedding. _____ (They/It) are all black and white photos.
5.
My mother and father look nervous, but _____ (I/me) am sure
6.
_____ (we/they) were very happy. The last part of the album is filled
7.
with pictures of _____ (my/me) and my baby brother. I think I look like
8.
my mother when _____ (she/her) was my age. I am so glad my
9.
grandparents made this album.

GRAMMAR GUIDE: POSSESSIVE ADJECTIVES

English has seven possessive adjectives. They are used before a noun to show ownership.

A. **Review the chart below.**

SINGULAR POSSESSIVE ADJECTIVES	EXAMPLES	PLURAL POSSESSIVE ADJECTIVES	EXAMPLES
my	**My** sisters are twins.	our	We sold **our** old furniture.
your	**Your** friend is nice.	your	This is **your** dictionary.
his, her, its	Drew is selling **his** car. Donna smiled at **her** mother.	their	The Ortegas painted **their** apartment.

B. **Complete each sentence with the correct possessive adjective.**

1. I like to spend time with _____ brothers.

2. My sister loves _____ new puppy.

3. My parents love _____ children.

4. Daniel likes to play games on _____ computer.

5. Suzanne and Gary enjoy playing with _____ cousins.

6. Mrs. Lee works out of _____ house.

C. **Complete the paragraph with the correct possessive adjectives.**

I live with _____ Uncle Steve and _____ family in
 _{1.}   _{2.}
Boulder, Colorado. My uncle is a librarian. He works at the Norlin Library at the University
of Colorado. My uncle got married two years ago. _____ wife is very nice.
 _{3.}
_____ name is Patricia. She is a photographer. Now she is a mother, too. Last
 _{4.}
week, _____ aunt and uncle had a baby girl. _____ name is
 _{5.}   _{6.}
Anna. I'm very happy to be an aunt.

WRITING ABOUT YOUR OWN FAMILY

Prewriting

A. **Show your family tree to a partner and use it to describe your family.**

B. **Answer these questions about your family.**

1. How many people are there in your family? _____

2. What are your parents' names? _____

   Where do they live? _____

3. What does your father do? _____

   What does your mother do? _____

4. How many brothers and sisters do you have? _____

   What are their names? _____

   How old are they? _____

5. Do you have any children? _____ How many? _____

   What are their names? _____

   How old are they? _____

Writing

A. **Write at least five sentences about your family.**

1. _____

2. _____

3. _____

4. _____

5. _____

B. Use your sentences to write a paragraph about your family. Begin by choosing an adjective to complete the first sentence. Remember to follow the rules of paragraph writing. Use at least three pronouns in your paragraph. Give your paragraph a title.

_____

I have a _____ family. (big/small/happy) _____

_____

_____

_____

_____

_____

_____

Revising

A. Exchange paragraphs with a partner. Read the paragraph your partner wrote. Then use the Revising Checklist to help your partner improve his or her paragraph.

REVISING CHECKLIST	YES	NO
1. Is the first word of the paragraph indented?		
2. Does each sentence begin with a capital letter and end with correct punctuation?		
3. Does each new sentence begin next to the one before it?		
4. Are there at least three pronouns?		
5. Does the paragraph have a good title?		

B. Use your partner's suggestions to revise your own paragraph on a separate piece of paper. Put it in your portfolio.

WRITING ABOUT A RELATIVE

Prewriting

A. Think about someone in your family you would like to write about.

Write your relative's name here: _____

B. Answer these questions about your relative.

1. How is this person related to you (cousin, sister, brother, etc.)? _____

2. How old is he or she? _____

3. Is he or she married or single? _____

4. Where does he or she live? _____

5. What does he or she do? _____

6. What is one thing he or she likes to do? _____

7. What is one more thing he or she likes to do? _____

C. **Write one or two more interesting things about your relative.**

_____

_____

Writing

A. **Write five sentences about your relative.**

1. _____

2. _____

3. _____

4. _____

5. _____

B. **Use your sentences to write a paragraph about your relative. Use at least three pronouns in your paragraph. Give your paragraph a title.**

_____

My _____ 's name is _____

_____

_____

_____

_____

Revising

A. **Exchange paragraphs with a partner. Read the paragraph your partner wrote. Then use the Revising Checklist to help your partner improve his or her paragraph.**

REVISING CHECKLIST		
	YES	**NO**
1. Is the first word of the paragraph indented?		
2. Does each sentence begin with a capital letter and end with correct punctuation?		
3. Does each new sentence begin next to the one before it?		
4. Are there at least three pronouns?		
5. Does the paragraph have a good title?		

B. Use your partner's suggestions and your own ideas to revise your paragraph on a separate piece of paper. Put it in your portfolio.

GRAMMAR GUIDE: *AND, BUT*

When you write in English you can connect words and sentences using *and* and *but* to make your writing more interesting. These words are called conjunctions.

A. Study the chart below.

CONJUNCTION	USE	EXAMPLE
and	joins two similar ideas together	Tom Brower has a close family, **and** he loves them very much.
but	joins two contrasting ideas	Sandra enjoys spending time with her family, **but** she doesn't get to see them very often.

B. Combine the pairs of sentences using *and* or *but*.

1. Sandra goes out with her cousins. She goes out with her friends, too.

   _____

2. Maria would like to spend more time with her sisters. She is usually too busy.

   _____

3. Erin wants to e-mail her mother. Her computer is broken.

   _____

4. Min sent in her application. She is waiting for the result.

   _____

5. My aunt is from Turkey. My uncle is from Turkey, too.

   _____

C. Compare your sentences with a partner's. Did you use the same words to combine the sentences?

D. Read the paragraph and circle the conjunctions.

My Best Friend

My best friend's name is José. He is very responsible, and he is also fun to be with. We have a great time whenever we get together. He is smart, and he reads a lot. That's why he always has interesting things to say. He is quite a talkative guy, but he is a very good listener, too. I can talk about my problems with him, and he always gives me good advice. I am really glad to have a friend like José.

WRITING ABOUT A FRIEND

Prewriting

A. **In small groups, discuss the qualities of a good friend. Put a check (✔) next to the qualities that you think are important.**

_____ responsible   _____ good listener   _____ loyal

_____ fun to be with   _____ honest   _____ friendly

_____ kind   _____ good-looking   _____ helpful

_____ intelligent   _____ wealthy   _____ generous

B. **Choose a friend to write about. Describe your friend to the people in your group. What qualities does your friend have?**

Write your friend's name here: _____

C. **Answer the questions about your friend.**

1. How old is your friend? _____

2. Is your friend married or single? _____

3. Where does he or she live? _____

4. What does your friend do? _____

5. What does he or she like to do? _____

6. What qualities does your friend have? _____

D. **Write one or two more interesting facts about your friend.**

_____

_____

Writing

A. **Write six sentences about your friend.**

1. _____

2. _____

3. _____

4. _____

5. _____

6. _____

B. Use some of your sentences to write a paragraph about your friend. Remember to follow the rules of paragraph writing. Use at least three pronouns and three conjunctions in your paragraph. Give your paragraph a title.

_____

My friend's name is _____

_____

_____

_____

_____

_____

Revising

A. Exchange paragraphs with a partner. Read the paragraph your partner wrote. Then use the Revising Checklist to help your partner improve his or her paragraph.

REVISING CHECKLIST	YES	NO
1. Is the first word of the paragraph indented?		
2. Does each sentence begin with a capital letter and end with correct punctuation?		
3. Does each new sentence begin next to the one before it?		
4. Are there at least three pronouns?		
5. Are there at least three conjunctions?		
6. Does the paragraph have a good title?		

B. Use your partner's suggestions to revise your paragraph on a separate piece of paper. Put it in your portfolio.

ON YOUR OWN

Choose one of the following topics. When you are done with your first draft, use the Revising Checklist to improve your paragraph.

- Write a paragraph about another friend. Use the questions on page 23 to help you get started.
- Talk to one of your younger relatives. Write a paragraph about him or her.
- Talk to one of your older relatives. Write a paragraph about him or her.
- Write about someone you met recently. Where did you meet him or her?
- Think about someone you miss. Write a paragraph about that person.

USE YOUR IMAGINATION

A. Pretend it is the year 2030. Make a list of sentences about your family. Think about their children, careers, and homes; predict how this may change.

Examples:

> I have a son named Stephen. He is a math teacher.
>
> My daughter's name is Diana. She is the mayor of my hometown.

1. _____
2. _____
3. _____
4. _____
5. _____

B. Choose an adjective such as *wonderful, small, large,* or *unusual* to describe your "future" family, and complete the first sentence. Then use your sentences from Exercise A to write a paragraph.

> I have a(n) _____ family. _____

_____

_____

_____

_____

YOU BE THE EDITOR

The paragraph below has five mistakes with pronouns. With a partner, find and correct the mistakes.

My Cousin

My cousin's name is Bettina Lee. She is thirty-seven years old. She was born in Chicago, Illinois, but now her lives in Denver, Colorado. She is married and has two children. Bettina and me enjoy spending time together. Us love to go ice-skating. Bettina is an excellent ice-skater. She skated in ice shows when he was young. Now Bettina teaches ice-skating to young children. She enjoys watching their.

An E-mail Message

Writing e-mail messages is a quick and easy way to communicate. E-mails are usually short and specific.

A. Read the sample e-mail.

Send	Reply	Forward	Move	Print	Delete	▲ ▼

To:	Sharon
From:	Christina
Subject:	Birthday Lunch

Hi Sharon,

Diane, Nina, and I want to take you out for lunch for your birthday. Are you free for fine food and fun on Friday? We'll pick you up at noon.

Let me know if this works for you.

Love,
Christina

B. Write an e-mail for each of the following situations.

1. Write an e-mail to your roommate, Juanita. Remind her to stop at the pizza shop on her way home and get a large mushroom pizza.

Send	Reply	Forward	Move	Print	Delete	▲ ▼

To:	
From:	
Subject:	

2. Write an e-mail to your friend Paul. Tell him that you are sorry, but you will not be able to meet him for dinner tonight. Ask him if tomorrow night is good for him.

Send	Reply	Forward	Move	Print	Delete	▲	▼

To:

From:

Subject:

3. Write an e-mail to your coworker Jong. Tell him your car broke down. Ask him to give you a ride to work tomorrow morning.

Send	Reply	Forward	Move	Print	Delete	▲	▼

To:

From:

Subject:

WRITING ABOUT YOUR ACTIVITIES

WRITING ABOUT ACTIVITIES YOU LIKE

A. Look at the five pictures. They show activities a student named Eric likes to do with his friends. Write the name of the activity under the correct picture. Use words from the word bank.

ACTIVITIES WORD BANK

go out to dinner	go to the movies	play video games
go to concerts	play soccer	

1. _____

2. _____

3. _____

4. _____

5. _____

B. Read the paragraph about what Eric likes to do in his free time.

Spending Time with Friends

In his free time, Eric likes to do things with his friends. He often plays soccer with his friends after class. On the weekends, he likes to go out to dinner or go see a movie with them. Eric and his friends go to concerts, too. Sometimes they don't go anywhere, but they aren't bored. They play video games, or they just sit around and talk and laugh. Eric always has fun when he is with his friends.

C. Talk to a partner. Ask and answer these questions.

1. What does Eric like to do in his free time?
2. What do Eric and his friends like to play after class?
3. What else does Eric like to do with his friends?

GRAMMAR GUIDE: THE SIMPLE PRESENT

We use the simple present to write about daily activities and things that are usually true.

A. Draw a circle around the subject of each sentence. Underline the verb.

1. I ride my bike for exercise.
2. She plants many kinds of flowers in her garden.
3. It snows a lot here in January.
4. They watch TV in the evenings.
5. We play tennis every weekend.
6. Pam and Lisa eat lunch in the cafeteria.
7. He collects stamps from all over the world.
8. You play the piano very well.
9. Chris listens to music on his iPod.

B. Look at the sentences again. Which subjects use the base form of the verb? Write them.

_____   _____

_____   _____

_____

_____

_____

_____

D. **Work with a partner. Complete the two rules.**

1. We use the **-s** form of the verb when the subject of the sentence is _____

    _____

2. We use the base form of the verb when the subject of the sentence is _____

    _____

Forming the Simple Present

A. **Study the spelling rules for forming simple present verbs.**

VERB ENDING	EXAMPLES
Most verbs: add **-s**	work → work**s** play → play**s**
Consonant + _y_: change the **y** to **i** and add **-es**	wor**ry** → worr**ies**
_s, z, ch, sh_, and _x_: add **-es**	tou**ch** → touch**es**

Some verbs are irregular. You need to learn the forms for the simple present of these verbs. Here are some examples: _go/goes, do/does,_ and _have/has._

B. **Two common verbs, _be_ and _have,_ form the simple present in an irregular way. Read the sentences with the verb _be._ Circle the verb and then answer the questions.**

a. I am a student.

b. You are a student.

c. He is the teacher.

d. Sam is a businessman.

e. She is a doctor.

f. The window is open.

g. It is an old house.

h. We are from England.

i. You are students.

j. They are tired.

k. Jane and Chris are from Toronto.

1. Which subject uses _am_? _____

2. Which subjects use _is_? _____

3. Which subjects use _are_? _____

C. Now study the sentences that use the verb *have*. Circle the verb in each sentence. Then complete the two rules.

a. I have two brothers.

b. You have a headache.

c. He has a new car.

d. Isabelle has long hair.

e. She has lots of friends.

f. The book has ten chapters.

g. It has a red cover.

h. We have tickets to the movie.

i. You have a beautiful home.

j. They have three children.

k. Lance and Robin have twins.

1. We use **has** when the subject of the sentence is _____

   _____

2. We use **have** when the subject of the sentence is _____

   _____

Forming Negatives

A. Study the rules for forming negatives of simple present verbs.

RULE	EXAMPLES
Add **does not/doesn't** before the base form of the verb for the third person singular.	He **doesn't** work.
Add **do not/don't** for plural subjects *I, you,* and *they*.	They **don't** have a car. I **don't** have a car. You **don't** have a car.
Add the word **not** after the verb **be**.	I **am not** hungry. (I**'m not** hungry.) You **are not** late. (You **aren't** late.) He **is not** a doctor. (He **isn't** a doctor.) She **is not** a student. (She **isn't** a student.) It **is not** my car. (It **isn't** my car.) We **are not** married. (We **aren't** married.) They **are not** from Brazil. (They **aren't** from Brazil.)

B. Underline the simple present verbs in the paragraph "Spending Time with Friends" on page 29.

C. The sentences below have mistakes with simple present verbs. Correct the sentences.

1. Maria don't worry about her children.

   _____

2. We plays soccer on the weekend.

   _____

3. You is never on time.

   _____

4. She wash her clothes every week.

   _____

5. Both of my sisters lives in Texas.

   _____

6. I has lots of new friends in my class.

   _____

7. I no think he watches too much TV.

   _____

8. She have a lot of friends.

   _____

9. He don't like coffee.

   _____

10. They doesn't have a big house.

    _____

D. **Rewrite the paragraph. Change *I* to *Shelly*. Change the verbs and pronouns as necessary.**

> I like to spend my free time outdoors. My favorite outdoor activity is gardening, and I love to plant new kinds of flowers in my garden every year. I also enjoy taking long walks in the park and riding my bike. On sunny days, I go to the beach with my friends. As you can see, I love being outside in my free time.

Shelly likes to spend her free time outdoors.

_____

_____

_____

_____

_____

PARTS OF A PARAGRAPH

In Chapter 1 you learned that a paragraph is a group of sentences that communicates one main idea. Most paragraphs have three parts: a **topic sentence**, several **supporting sentences**, and a **concluding sentence**.

The **topic sentence** is the most important sentence in the paragraph. It is often the first sentence in the paragraph. The topic sentence tells the reader what the paragraph is about.

Next come the **supporting sentences**. These sentences give details, examples, and reasons to explain the topic sentence. All of the supporting sentences must relate to the topic of the paragraph.

Some paragraphs end with a **concluding sentence**. The concluding sentence restates the main idea in different words. Here are some common ways to begin a concluding sentence: *All in all, As you can see, In conclusion.*

PARAGRAPH POINTER: Paragraph Structure

It may be helpful to think of a paragraph as a sandwich. The topic and concluding sentences are like the top and bottom pieces of bread. The supporting sentences are like the lettuce, tomatoes, cheese, and meat that you put between the pieces of bread.

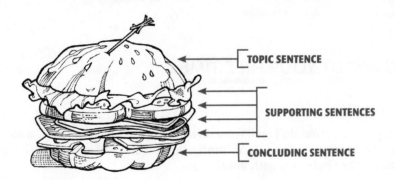

Work with a partner. Read each paragraph and think about the parts. Ask and answer the questions that follow.

1.   I love to play games. I enjoy games that you play with other people, such as card games and board games. I especially like games that make you think hard. That's why my favorite game is chess. I also like games that you can play alone, such as solitaire and sudoku. Naturally, I like playing games on the computer, too. All in all, I think games are fun and challenging.

   a. What is the topic sentence? Circle it.
   b. How many supporting sentences are there? _____
   c. What is the concluding sentence? Underline it.

2. I have several hobbies that keep me busy in my free time. I love to read, and I often read short stories and magazines. Another one of my hobbies is cooking, and Chinese cooking is my specialty. My favorite hobby is photography. I usually take black-and-white pictures because I think they are more interesting than color pictures. In conclusion, my life would not be as much fun without my hobbies.

   a. What is the topic sentence? Circle it.
   b. How many supporting sentences are there? _____
   c. What is the concluding sentence? Underline it.

3. I live in a big city, so there are many things to do in my free time. One thing I really enjoy is trying different kinds of restaurants. I also like going to concerts and listening to new bands. Even if I don't have any extra money, I love to go shopping. Sometimes, I just like to sit at a café and watch people. With so many choices, I often have a hard time deciding what to do in my free time.

   a. What is the topic sentence? Circle it.
   b. How many supporting sentences are there? _____
   c. What is the concluding sentence? Underline it.

WRITING ABOUT YOUR FREE TIME

Prewriting

A. **Talk to a partner. What do you like to do in your free time? Discuss some things that you like to do with your friends or family. What things do you like to do alone? Use the word bank to help you with vocabulary.**

FREE-TIME ACTIVITIES WORD BANK		
bake/cook	go to museums	play sports (golf, tennis, soccer, etc.)
collect (stamps, comic books, etc.)	go to parties	read
	listen to music	
dance	paint	sew/knit
draw	play an instrument (guitar, piano, flute)	sing
exercise/work out		swim/ski/surf
fly kites	play computer/video games	take pictures
go see a movie		take walks
go shopping	play games (chess, backgammon)	talk on the phone
go to concerts		

B. **Make a list of the activities you like to do in your free time.**

_____   _____

_____   _____

_____   _____

C. **Share your list with your partner. Talk about the activities you like the most. Do you and your partner like to do any of the same things? Which ones?**

Writing

A. **Use your list to complete each of the sentences.**

1. I like to _____

2. I also like to _____

3. Another thing I enjoy is _____

4. I like to _____, and I _____

5. I enjoy _____, but I _____

B. **Use your sentences to write a paragraph. Complete the topic sentence. Then write three or four supporting sentences, and complete the concluding sentence. Add a title.**

_____

In my free time, I _____

_____

_____

_____

As you can see, _____

Revising

A. **Exchange paragraphs with a partner. Read the paragraph your partner wrote. Then use the Revising Checklist to help your partner improve his or her paragraph.**

REVISING CHECKLIST		
	YES	**NO**
1. Does each sentence begin with a capital letter and end with correct punctuation?		
2. Does each new sentence begin next to the one before it?		
3. Is there a topic sentence?		
4. Are there three or four supporting sentences?		
5. Does the concluding sentence restate the main idea?		

B. **Use your partner's suggestions to revise your paragraph on a separate piece of paper. Put it in your portfolio.**

Prewriting

Work in a small group. Complete the chart with each person's favorite free-time activities.

NAME	FAVORITE FREE-TIME ACTIVITIES

Writing

A. Write three sentences based on the information in the chart.

1. _____

2. _____

3. _____

B. Use your sentences to complete the paragraph. Include three or four supporting sentences. Complete the concluding sentence.

The people in my group like to do many things in their free time. _____

_____

_____

_____

_____

As you can see, _____

Revising

A. Use the Revising Checklist to help you improve your paragraph.

REVISING CHECKLIST	YES	NO
1. Does each sentence begin with a capital letter and end with correct punctuation?		
2. Does each new sentence begin next to the one before it?		
3. Is there a topic sentence?		
4. Are there three or four supporting sentences?		
5. Does the concluding sentence restate the main idea?		

B. Exchange paragraphs with a partner. Read the paragraph your partner wrote. Then use the Revising Checklist to help your partner improve his or her paragraph.

A. **Look at the pictures. They show activities that people do to stay healthy. Discuss the pictures with a partner. Use the words and phrases from the word bank.**

HEALTHY ACTIVITIES WORD BANK		
does yoga	gets checkups	rides (his or her) bike
eats nutritious foods	gets eight hours of sleep	works out

B. **Complete the sentences.**

1. Ari _____ , such as fruits and vegetables, to stay healthy.

2. Sally _____ two miles to school every day.

3. Sam _____ at his doctor's office at least once a year.

4. Mary always _____ a night.

5. Janice _____ at the gym four times a week.

6. Cassie _____ every evening to relax.

C. **Read the paragraph. Underline the topic sentence and the concluding sentence. Circle the simple present verbs.**

Staying Healthy

I do several things to stay healthy. First of all, I exercise regularly. I work out at the gym four times a week. I also ride my bike to school and play tennis on the weekends. In addition, I am careful about my diet. For example, I eat lots of fruits and vegetables, and I avoid junk food. I also try to get eight hours of sleep every night. Most importantly, I quit smoking! Like many of my friends, staying healthy is important to me.

WRITING ABOUT YOUR HEALTHY ACTIVITIES

Prewriting

A. **Work with a group of three or four students. Discuss the questions.**

1. Do you exercise regularly? How often do you exercise?
2. What kind of exercises do you do?
3. Do you eat healthy meals? What kinds of food do you think are good for you? What kinds of food do you think are not very good for you?
4. Do you smoke? If so, how much and when do you smoke?
5. Do you usually get enough sleep at night? How many hours of sleep do you usually get? How much sleep do you need?

B. **Think of five more ways to stay healthy. Add your ideas to the list.**

Ways to Stay Healthy

1. Do not smoke cigarettes. _____
2. _____
3. _____
4. _____
5. _____
6. _____

C. **Compare your list with another group's. Did you have any of the same ideas? Which ones were the same?**

Writing

A. **Choose one of these topic sentences.**

1. I do several things to try to stay healthy.
2. There are several ways to stay healthy.

B. **Write a paragraph. Use some of the ideas from your list for at least three supporting sentences. End your paragraph with a concluding sentence. Add a title.**

_____

_____

_____

_____

_____

_____

_____

Revising

A. **Exchange paragraphs with a partner. Read the paragraph your partner wrote. Then use the Revising Checklist to help your partner improve his or her paragraph.**

REVISING CHECKLIST	YES	NO
1. Does each sentence begin with a capital letter and end with correct punctuation?		
2. Does each new sentence begin next to the one before it?		
3. Are there at least three supporting sentences?		
4. Is there a concluding sentence?		

B. **Use your partner's suggestions to revise your paragraph on a separate piece of paper. Put it in your portfolio.**

ON YOUR OWN

Choose one of the following topics. When you are done with your first draft, use the Revising Checklist to improve your paragraph.

- Talk to someone in your family about what he or she likes to do in his or her free time. Write a paragraph about how that person spends his or her free time.
- Talk to someone in your family or one of your friends about what he or she does to stay healthy. Write a paragraph about how that person stays healthy.
- Find someone who has an unusual hobby or interest. Write about what that person likes to do in his or her free time.

YOU BE THE EDITOR

The paragraph below has seven mistakes with simple present verbs. With a partner, find and correct the mistakes.

A Tired New Mother

I am a proud but tired mother of twin baby boys. I don't has any free time these days. My days am very busy, and my nights are busy, too. I never gets much sleep anymore. I wake up several times during the night to feed the babies. They have always hungry! So, I am tired in the morning. I try to take naps when the babies are napping, but I have so much to do. I wash baby clothes and blankets every morning and evening. I also changes diapers all day long. Sometimes when both babies cries at the same time, I cry, too. But when I watches them sleeping peacefully, I know how lucky I am to have two happy, healthy babies.

A. Write an e-mail to your friend. Describe an activity, such as a movie, concert, restaurant, or party, that you plan to go to. Invite your friend to join you.

Send	Reply	Forward	Save	Print	✕ Discard	▲ ▼

To:

Subject:

B *I* <u>U</u>   Times New Roman ☐

B. Exchange your e-mail with a partner. Write a response to your partner's e-mail.

Send	Reply	Forward	Save	Print	✕ Discard	▲ ▼

To:

Subject:

B *I* <u>U</u>   Times New Roman ☐

GIVING INSTRUCTIONS

WRITING ABOUT HOW TO MAKE OR DO SOMETHING

A. **Look at the pictures. They show the steps to make a yogurt milkshake. Read the steps. Match each step to the correct picture. Write the letter.**

1. _____

2. _____

3. _____

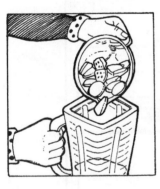

4. _____

5. _____

6. _____

a. Then cut up some fresh fruit such as bananas, peaches, mangoes, or strawberries.

b. First, get out 1 cup of yogurt, 2 cups of milk, and 2 tablespoons of honey.

c. Add the fruit to the yogurt, milk, and honey in the blender.

d. Pour the yogurt, milk, and honey into a blender.

e. Finally, pour the milkshake into glasses and enjoy your nutritious snack.

f. Put the top on the blender and blend on medium for two minutes.

B. Use the steps to complete a paragraph about how to make a yogurt milkshake.

How to Make a Yogurt Milkshake

When you want a delicious and healthy snack, try this yogurt milkshake.

_____

_____

_____

_____

Once you see how easy it is to make a yogurt milkshake and taste how delicious it is, you'll want to share the recipe with your friends.

GRAMMAR GUIDE: COUNT NOUNS AND NONCOUNT NOUNS

There are two kinds of nouns in English: *count nouns* and *noncount nouns*. Learning which nouns are count and which are noncount can be very difficult for students learning English. A noun that is a noncount noun in English may be a count noun in another language. Another problem is that some nouns in English can be count or noncount depending on the situation.

Count Nouns

Count nouns are nouns that you can count: one cup, two pencils, five chairs, twenty-seven students. Count nouns have a singular form and a plural form.

We use *a* or *an* before singular count nouns. Use *a* with singular count nouns that begin with a consonant sound. Use *an* with singular count nouns that begin with a vowel sound.

A. Complete each sentence with *a* or *an*.

1. Can I borrow _____ eraser?

2. He gave me _____ present for my birthday.

3. Cut up _____ apple.

4. Did you have _____ snack?

5. I have _____ aunt who lives in Sidney, Australia and _____ uncle who lives in Wellington, New Zealand.

6. I'm saving my money to buy _____ new cell phone that takes pictures.

7. My friend was taken to the hospital in _____ ambulance after the car accident.

8. I have _____ headache so I took _____ aspirin.

Most count nouns form the plural by adding -s or -es, but others require spelling changes.

B. **Study the chart below.**

TYPE OF NOUN	HOW TO FORM THE PLURAL	EXAMPLES
Most nouns	Add **-s**.	banana → bananas cup → cups snack → snacks
Nouns that end in *ch, s, sh, ss,* and *x*	Add **-es**.	lun**ch** → lunches wi**sh** → wishes cla**ss** → classes
Nouns that end in a consonant + *y*	Change the **y** to **i** and add **-es**.	ber**ry** → berries ci**ty** → cities fami**ly** → families
Nouns that end in *o*	Add **-es**.	mang**o** → mangoes potat**o** → potatoes tomat**o** → tomatoes
Nouns that end in *f*	Change **f** to **v** and add **-es**.	hal**f** → halves wol**f** → wolves *Exception:* roo**f** → roofs
Nouns that end in *fe*	Change **f** to **v** and add **-s**.	kni**fe** → knives li**fe** → lives wi**fe** → wives

In addition, there are irregular plural forms of count nouns.

child → children	man → men	person → people	tooth → teeth
foot → feet	mouse → mice	radio → radios	woman → women

C. **Underline the plural nouns in the paragraph "How to Make a Yogurt Milkshake."**

D. **Complete the sentences. Use the plural form of a word from the list.**

child	knife	potato	tooth
glass	loaf	strawberry	

1. I drank two _____glasses_____ of milk.

2. She added some _____ to her milkshake.

3. You need to peel all the _____ before you boil them.

4. I baked three _____ of bread.

5. Keep the sharp _____ away from the _____.

6. I brush my _____ after every meal.

Noncount Nouns

Noncount nouns are things that we can't or don't usually count. Noncount nouns do not have singular or plural forms. They always take the verb form used with singular nouns.

We do not use *a* or *an* with noncount nouns. Instead, we use phrases with noncount nouns that tell us quantity, such as *a lot of*, *a little*, *some*, *any*, *much*, *two cups of*, and *one teaspoon of*.

It is very difficult to learn all of the noncount nouns in English.

Examples:

I put **some** *sugar* in my coffee.

He likes **a little** *milk* in his tea.

We have **a lot of** *homework*.

A. **Study the chart with categories and examples of common noncount nouns.**

CATEGORIES	EXAMPLES
food	bread, butter, cheese, chicken, fish, flour, pepper, rice, salt, sugar
liquid	coffee, juice, milk, soda, soup, tea, water
subjects	chemistry, English, history, math, music
abstract ideas	anger, beauty, humor, justice, knowledge, love, luck
others	furniture, homework, information, money, software

B. **Read the sentences. Correct the mistakes. One sentence is correct. Circle it.**

1. I am studying a chemistry.

2. I bought some new furnitures.

3. I did my homeworks last night.

4. He added some salt to the soup.

5. Do you have an information about the movie?

6. The baby drinks a lot of milks every day.

TIME-ORDER SIGNAL WORDS

You have already learned several important things about paragraphs. You know that a paragraph has a special form. You also know that a paragraph has three parts: a topic sentence, supporting sentences, and a concluding sentence. It is also important to learn how to organize the supporting sentences. There are several common ways to do this. One way is to use time order. That means organizing your ideas in the order in which they happen.

Many paragraphs include signal words to connect ideas in a paragraph. Signal words help guide the reader from one idea to the next.

When you want to explain how to do something, the first thing you need to do is make a list of the steps in the process. Then you should arrange the steps according to time order. When you write your paragraph, use time-order signal words to make the order of the steps clear to the reader.

A. **Review the examples of time-order signal words.**

TIME-ORDER SIGNAL WORDS		
first	first of all	next
second	then	finally
third	after that	

B. **Look at the cartoon. Read the caption (the words under the picture) and underline the time-order signal words.**

Copyright © 1999 Randy Glasbergen

GLASBERGEN

"Licking your paws is just the first step.
After that, you need to use a good antibacterial
body wash, then an exfoliating herbal facial scrub,
followed by avocado moisturizing cleanser...."

C. **Complete the paragraphs using time-order signal words.**

1.   It's not hard to get a good picture of your cat if you follow these steps.

_____, give your cat something to eat. When she is full, move

your cat to a sunny window. _____, rub your cat's back for a few

minutes until she falls asleep. Do not make any loud noises. As soon as she wakes up,

get in position and have your camera ready. _____, take the picture

as she yawns and stretches.

2. In order to get a driver's license in the United States you need to follow these steps. _____, go to the Department of Motor Vehicles in the state where you live and fill out an application. _____, study for and take a written test on the traffic signs and driving laws. You also have to take and pass a vision test. _____, you need to take a road test. The person who gives you the test will make sure that you can drive safely. Once you pass the road test, you will get your driver's license.

3. It's easy to get driving directions from one place to another on the Internet using a site called *Live Search Maps*. _____, open *Live Search Maps* and click the icon that says "Directions." _____, type into the "Start" box the address or location where you will begin your trip. _____, type into the "End" box the address of your destination. At this point, you can choose your route. To choose the quickest way, click "Shortest Time." To choose the shortest way, click "Shortest Distance." _____, click "Get Directions" and you will get step-by-step directions from your starting point to your destination. Hopefully, you won't get lost.

GRAMMAR GUIDE: IMPERATIVE SENTENCES

An imperative sentence expresses a command or a request. When we give someone instructions, we often use imperative sentences.

You have learned that a sentence must have a subject and a verb. In an imperative sentence the subject is always *you*, but it is not stated. Imperative sentences begin with the base form of a verb and end with a period or an exclamation point. Look at the examples. Notice that each one begins with a verb.

For negative imperative forms, we use: *Do + not* (OR *Don't*) + base form of the verb.

STATEMENTS	**Press** the start button.
	Close the door.
	Add the sugar.
	Go to the Department of Motor Vehicles in the state where you live and fill out an application.
	Slow down!
NEGATIVE STATEMENTS	**Do not** *make* any loud noises.
	Do not *let* the water boil.
	Don't *add* too much salt.

A. **Circle the imperative verbs in the paragraph "How to Make a Yogurt Milkshake" on page 43.**

B. Underline the imperative verbs in the paragraphs that follow.

1.　　　Here are several steps you can follow to avoid jet lag. First of all, get a good night's sleep the night before you travel. Secondly, set your watch to the time of your destination when you get on the plane. Then, drink plenty of water during the flight. Don't drink alcohol or caffeine. Also, move around during the flight. Walk around the plane or do some simple stretching exercises in your seat. When you arrive at your destination, keep busy. Do not take a nap. Eat meals and go to bed when the local people do.

2.　　　You can make perfect hard-boiled eggs if you follow these steps. First, take the eggs out of the refrigerator before cooking and let them come to room temperature. Then, put the eggs in a pan with enough water to cover them by at least an inch. Bring the water to a boil. Turn off the heat as soon as the water boils and cover the eggs for about 15 minutes. Next, put the eggs in a bowl with cold water and a few ice cubes. Let the eggs cool for 10 minutes. Now you are ready to peel the eggs and enjoy eating them.

Activity 1

A. Discuss the pictures with a partner. Then number the steps in time order.

How to Remove an Ink Stain

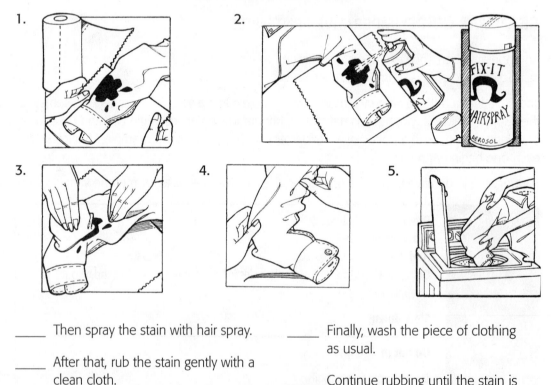

_____ Then spray the stain with hair spray.

_____ After that, rub the stain gently with a clean cloth.

_____ First, put a paper towel under the stain.

_____ Finally, wash the piece of clothing as usual.

_____ Continue rubbing until the stain is completely gone.

B. **Read the topic sentence. Then use the steps in Exercise A to complete the paragraph.**

This is what you need to do to remove an ink stain from clothing.

_____

_____

_____

_____

_____

Activity 2

A. **Discuss the pictures with a partner. Then number the steps in time order.**

How to Stop a Nosebleed

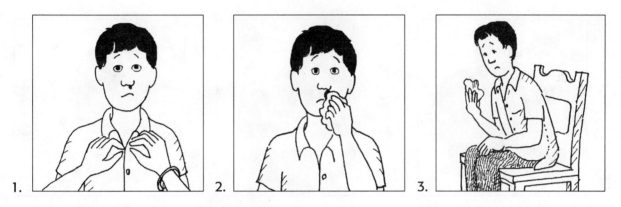

1.   2.   3.

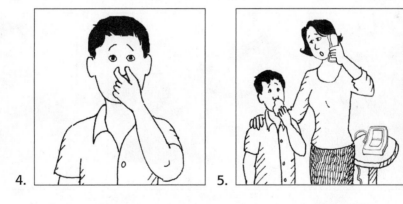

4.   5.

_____ Put a cotton pad in the bleeding nostril.

_____ Squeeze your nose until it stops bleeding.

_____ If your nose continues to bleed, call a doctor.

_____ Then, sit down with your head leaning forward.

_____ First, loosen the clothing around your neck.

B. Read the topic sentence. Then use the steps from Exercise A on page 49 to complete the paragraph.

You should follow these steps to stop a nosebleed.

_____

_____

_____

_____

Activity 3

A. Discuss the pictures with a partner. They show how to carve a pumpkin. Read the list of steps. Then number the steps in time order.

How to Carve a Pumpkin

1.

2.

3.

4.

5.

6.

7.

_____ Next, draw a pattern for the face on the pumpkin with a felt-tip pen.

_____ Then, gently push out the cut-out features to the inside of the pumpkin.

_____ Finally, place a small candle inside the pumpkin.

_____ First you need to make a lid. To do this, draw a circle about 6 inches in diameter on top of the pumpkin around the stem.

_____ Use a smaller knife to carefully carve out the face you drew on your pumpkin.

_____ Then, use a large, sharp knife to cut around the circle and remove the lid.

_____ After that, scoop out the seeds and pulp from inside the pumpkin with a large spoon.

B.   Use the steps from Exercise A to complete the paragraph.

Carving a pumpkin for Halloween is fun, but it is also messy. So, make sure you have covered your work area with newspaper before you begin.

_____

_____

_____

_____

_____

_____

_____

_____

_____

_____

_____

WRITING ABOUT HOW TO MAKE OR DO SOMETHING

Prewriting

A.   Choose one of the following topics to write about.
   * how to send an e-mail
   * how to pack for a weekend trip
   * how to make a good salad
   * how to fall asleep
   * how to mend a broken heart
   * how to cure the hiccups
   * how to treat a cold
   * how to convert from Celsius to Fahrenheit (or other metric to English measurements)

B. Make a list of all the steps in the process. The steps don't have to be in order.

_____ _____

_____ _____

_____ _____

_____ _____

_____ _____

_____ _____

C. Number the steps according to time order.

Writing

A. Write the steps from Exercise B above in sentence form. Use imperative sentences.

1. _____

2. _____

3. _____

4. _____

5. _____

6. _____

B. Complete this topic sentence about your process.

It is _____ to _____.
        (easy/fun/hard, etc.)

C. Write a paragraph giving instructions. Use the list of steps from Exercise A as a guide. Remember to begin with a topic sentence. Also, include time-order signal words to help guide your reader. Write a title for your paragraph.

_____

_____

_____

_____

_____

_____

_____

_____

_____

_____

_____

Revising

A. Exchange paragraphs with a partner. Read the paragraph your partner wrote. Then use the Revising Checklist to help your partner improve his or her paragraph.

REVISING CHECKLIST	YES	NO
1. Is there a topic sentence?		
2. Are the sentences in correct time order?		
3. Are there signal words to help guide the reader?		

B. Share your paragraph with your classmates. Put your instruction paragraph in your portfolio.

ON YOUR OWN

Choose one of the following topics. Then write a process paragraph on a separate piece of paper. Give your paragraph a title and put it in your portfolio.

- how to clean something (your room, your car, etc.)
- how to fix something (a flat tire, a broken vase, etc.)
- how to cook or bake something
- how to play something (checkers, soccer, etc.)
- one of the other paragraph topics from the list on page 51

YOU BE THE EDITOR

The paragraph below has six mistakes with singular and plural nouns. With a partner, find and correct the mistakes.

A Delicious Drink

Turkish coffee is not easy to make, but it is delicious. There are several way to make Turkish coffee, but this is the way my friend taught me. First, you will need a special pot called a *cezve*. Pour 3 cups of cold waters into the pot. Then, add 3 teaspoons of coffee and 3 teaspoons of sugars to the water. Next, heat the water on a low flame until you can see foam forming on top. Don't let it boil. Then take the pot off the heat. Gently stir the mixture and return it to the heat. Repeat this two more time. Finally, pour the coffee into 3 cups. Make sure each people gets some foams and enjoy your coffee.

Writing a Recipe Card

A. Fill out a recipe card for one of your favorite dishes. First make a list of the ingredients. Then write the instructions for how to prepare the dish. Use words from the word bank to help you.

INGREDIENTS WORD BANK					
bake	chop	cut	grill	mix	sauté
boil	combine	fry	heat	peel	simmer
broil	cook	garnish	melt	pour	stir

Recipe for: _____

Ingredients: _____   _____

_____   _____

_____   _____

_____   _____

Instructions: _____

_____

_____

_____

_____

_____

_____

_____

B. Prepare the dish and bring it to class to share with your classmates. Put your recipe card in your portfolio.

C. After you have tried your classmates' dishes, pick your favorite one. Copy the recipe for that dish onto the recipe card below. Add the card to your portfolio.

Recipe for: _____

Ingredients: _____   _____

_____   _____

_____   _____

_____   _____

Instructions: _____

_____

_____

_____

_____

_____

_____

_____

WRITING ABOUT YOUR DAY

WRITING ABOUT A TYPICAL DAY

A. **Look at the pictures. They show a typical day in the life of a man named Roberto Trevino. Find the sentence on page 57 that matches each picture. Write the letter of the sentence under the correct picture.**

1. _____

2. _____

3. _____

4. _____

5. _____

6. _____

7. _____

8. _____

a. Roberto teaches from 8:30 A.M. to 3:30 P.M..

b. He wakes up at 7:00 A.M. to eat breakfast and get dressed.

c. Finally, Roberto goes to bed at midnight.

d. Then he takes the 7:45 A.M. train to the school where he teaches English.

e. At 6:00 P.M., he eats dinner with his wife.

f. He takes the train back home at 4:00 P.M.

g. He plays the saxophone from 8:00 to 10:00 P.M. Sometimes he sings, too.

h. At 7:30 P.M., he arrives at The Jazz Club.

B. Use the sentences about Roberto to complete a paragraph about a typical day in his life. The topic sentence and concluding sentences are given.

Roberto's days are very busy.

_____

_____

_____

_____

_____

_____

_____ _As you can see, Roberto has a very busy life._

GRAMMAR GUIDE: PREPOSITIONS OF TIME

It is important to use the correct preposition when you are writing about time.

A. Study the chart below.

PREPOSITION	TIME WORDS	EXAMPLES
on	+ day of the week + day of the week + part of a day + a specific date	I go to work **on** Monday. I take an English class **on** Monday night. She was born **on** April 30.
in	+ a month + a part of the day _Exception: at night_	She was born **in** April. I do my homework **in** the evening. I do my homework **at night**.
at	+ a specific time	My English class starts **at** 9:30.
from	+ a specific time or date to a specific time or date	Mr. Morimoto exercises **from** 5:30 **to** 6:30 every morning.
for	+ a period of time	He exercises **for** an hour.

B. **Complete the sentences with the correct preposition of time.**

1. Do you want to go to the movies _____ Sunday afternoon?

2. She is going to the dentist _____ Monday.

3. Mohammed goes to work _____ 9:00.

4. Cheng goes to school _____ the morning.

5. I sent the e-mail _____ January 29.

6. I studied _____ three hours.

7. I like to watch TV _____ night.

8. I have classes _____ 10:00 _____ 4:30.

9. The new semester starts _____ January.

10. He wakes up _____ 7:30 _____ the morning.

C. **Complete the paragraph with the correct prepositions of time.**

My days are very busy. I wake up _____ 6:30 A.M. and take my dog for a walk. Then I eat breakfast, get ready for school, and make my lunch. I usually ride my bike to school. I have classes _____ 9 A.M. _____ 3 P.M. Then, I study at the library _____ the afternoon. I also have a part-time job. I wash dishes at a restaurant near campus. I work _____ 6 P.M. _____ 9 P.M. The job is not bad. I like the people I work with. I also get a free dinner! _____ 9 P.M., I ride my bike home. I take my dog for another walk. Then I relax. I often watch TV _____ an hour. Sometimes, I read or listen to music. Finally, I get ready for bed.

GRAMMAR GUIDE: FREQUENCY ADVERBS

We use frequency adverbs to tell how often something happens. The most common frequency adverbs are *always*, *usually*, *often*, *sometimes*, *rarely*, *seldom*, and *never*. Remember to use the simple present when you use frequency adverbs to write about your daily activities.

Frequency adverbs usually come after the verb **be**.

Examples:

He *is* **always** tired in the morning.

I *am* **rarely** in a bad mood.

They *are* **usually** late for parties.

Frequency adverbs usually come before all other verbs.

Examples:

She **often** *stays up* late.

We **seldom** *go out* to eat.

We **always** *listen* to the news after dinner.

A. **Study the chart below.**

FREQUENCY ADVERBS	EXAMPLES
always (100% of the time)	I don't have a car. I **always** take the bus to work.
usually	He **usually** gets up at 7 A.M. He is **usually** on time for class.
often	We **often** go for a walk after dinner. We are **often** tired after our walk.
sometimes (50% of the time)	I **sometimes** drink coffee after dinner. I am **sometimes** late for work.
rarely	Meryl is on a diet. She **rarely** eats dessert.
seldom	Jeff **seldom** goes to bed before midnight. He is **seldom** tired before midnight.
never (0% of the time)	Suzanne is a vegetarian. She **never** eats meat.

B. **Read the paragraph. Underline the frequency adverbs.**

A Busy Doctor

Dr. Gary Lesneski is an obstetrician. An obstetrician is a doctor who delivers babies. Dr. Lesneski usually gets up at six thirty in the morning. He goes to his office at seven o'clock. His workdays are never typical, but they are always busy. He never knows what time a baby will be born. Sometimes babies are born in the afternoon. Sometimes they are born at night. Often he has to go to the hospital in the middle of the night. He rarely sleeps through an entire night without any interruptions. Dr. Lesneski loves his work, but he looks forward to his vacation in August.

C. **Work in groups of three or four. Complete the chart by writing a frequency adverb that tells how often you and the other people in your group do each activity.**

always	usually	often	sometimes	rarely	seldom	never

	YOUR NAME:	NAME:	NAME:	NAME:
get up early				
eat lunch at a restaurant				
take the bus to school or work				
study in the library				
take a nap in the afternoon				
watch TV in the evening				
am/is late for school or work				
surf the Internet				
go to bed late				
read the newspaper				

D. Write sentences based on information in the chart.

Examples:

I usually get up early.

Clara rarely eats lunch at a restaurant.

1. _____
2. _____
3. _____
4. _____
5. _____
6. _____
7. _____
8. _____
9. _____
10. _____

GRAMMAR GUIDE: *BEFORE* AND *AFTER*

You can combine sentences with *before* and *after* to show time order. Notice that we use a comma when we start a sentence with *Before* or *After*.

A. **Study the chart to learn how to combine these two sentences:**

First, I brush my teeth. Then, I go to bed.

TIME WORDS	EXAMPLES
before	**Before** I go to bed, I brush my teeth. I brush my teeth **before** I go to bed.
after	**After** I brush my teeth, I go to bed. I go to bed **after** I brush my teeth.

B. **Combine the pairs of sentences using *before*. Use a comma when necessary.**

1. First I wash my hands. Then I eat dinner.

   I wash my hands before I eat dinner.

2. First I do my homework. Then I watch TV.

   _____

3. First I go to the gym. Then I do my homework.

_____

4. First I eat breakfast. Then I read the newspaper.

_____

C. Combine the pairs of sentences using *after*. Use a comma when necessary.

1. First I get home from work. Then I take my dog for a walk.

_____

2. First I eat dinner. Then I wash the dishes.

_____

3. First I get to school. Then I have coffee with my friends.

_____

4. First I read my son a story. Then I put him to bed.

_____

D. Complete the sentences.

1. After I get dressed in the morning, I _____

2. After I get to school (work), I _____

3. Before I do my homework, I _____

4. Before I make dinner, I _____

E. Look at the cartoon. Underline the simple present verbs. Do you think the cartoon is funny? Why or why not?

Copyright © 2003 Randy Glasbergen

"On Mondays, I get ready to plan my week.
On Tuesdays, I plan my week. On Wednesdays,
I revise my plan for the week. On Thursdays, I put
my plan for the week into my computer. On Fridays,
I think about starting my plan for next week."

PARAGRAPH POINTER: Paragraph Unity

You have learned that a paragraph is about one main idea. All of the supporting sentences in a paragraph must be about the main idea in the topic sentence. A sentence that does not support the main idea does not belong in the paragraph. When all of the sentences support the main idea, the paragraph has unity.

A. Read the paragraph. Underline the topic sentence.

Boring Days

During the week, my days are boring. I get up at 7 A.M. every day. Then I get dressed for school. Even that is boring because I have to wear a uniform to school. I always have the same thing for breakfast, fruit and yogurt, because it's fast and healthy. I take the bus to school where I spend the next seven hours. My schedule of classes is the same every day. My Spanish teacher is from Mexico. After school, I take the bus home and practice my violin for an hour. Finally, I do my homework and study. Luckily, my weekends are much more exciting.

The topic sentence states the main idea of the paragraph. All of the other sentences should explain the idea that the student's days are boring. Which sentence does not support this idea?

The sentence *My Spanish teacher is from Mexico* is true, but it is not about the student's boring days. Cross out that sentence.

B. One sentence in each paragraph does not belong. Cross out that sentence.

1. I love the water. I learned how to swim when I was just five years old. I have two younger sisters. Swimming is one of my favorite activities to do in the water. I also like sailing on lakes and scuba diving in the ocean. Besides having fun in the water, I am interested in the plants and animals that live in water. That's why I am studying marine biology. As you can see, I have a passion for the water, and I hope one day I can work in or around it.

2. Ben is a very athletic person. He loves to play all types of sports. Ben's favorite sport is volleyball. He belongs to a volleyball club where he can play with other people. Ben also likes to run and swim for exercise. He belongs to a gym where he exercises at least four times a week. Ben also works at the library. Ben certainly keeps himself busy with all of the athletic activities he does during the week.

PARAGRAPH POINTER: Time Order

When you write a paragraph about your day or week, you should use time order to organize the sentences. Begin with what you do first. Then write about what you do second, and so on. You can use signal words to make the order clear to your reader.

A. Review the time-order signal words you learned in Chapter 4, along with some new ones.

TIME-ORDER SIGNAL WORDS		
after that	first of all	second
finally	later	then
first	next	third
after breakfast	after school	before work
in the morning	in the afternoon	in the evening

B. Read the sentences. Write *TS* for topic sentence. Then number the supporting sentences so they are in correct time order. Finally, write the sentences in paragraph form. Add your own concluding sentence.

1. _____ Every morning at 6:00 A.M. he goes to the flower market to buy flowers.

   _TS_ Mr. Park owns a busy flower shop.

   _____ Then he drives to his shop.

   _____ He works there from 9:00 A.M. to 4:00 P.M.

   _____ After the store closes, Mr. Park delivers flowers.

   _____

   _____

   _____

   _____

   _____

2. _____ Then I go to classes for about five hours.

   _____ My typical day is pretty busy.

   _____ After my classes, I go to work at the university library.

   _____ I wake up early so I can read the paper, eat breakfast, and check my e-mail.

   _____ At 7 P.M., I usually meet my friends for dinner.

3. _____ She spends every morning exercising at the gym.

_____ After school, she goes to work at a store from 5:00 P.M. to 9:00 P.M.

_____ Then she takes classes at the university in the afternoon.

_____ Maria is very active during the summer.

_____ When the store closes, Maria often goes out with her coworkers.

_C._ **Read the paragraph below.**

Lazy Sundays

I am usually very lazy on Sundays. I get up late, and I eat a big breakfast. After breakfast, I read the newspaper for a few hours. Sometimes I talk to my friends on the telephone. At four o'clock, I am usually hungry, so I make a snack. Then I watch TV or take a nap. In the evening, I often go out to dinner with my friends, but I am back in bed again at ten o'clock. I like to relax on Sunday so that I am ready to start my week on Monday.

1. Draw a circle around the topic sentence of the paragraph.
2. Underline the supporting sentences.
3. Draw a circle around the concluding sentence of the paragraph.

_D._ **Rewrite the paragraph. Change _I_ to _Paulo_. Make all the other necessary changes.**

Paulo is _____

_____

_____

_____

_____

Prewriting

A. Draw simple pictures that show what you do on a typical weekday. Fill in the clock with the time you wake up.

B. Talk to a partner. Ask and answer questions about your typical weekday. Use your drawings to describe your typical day.

Writing

A. Write a sentence to go with each picture you drew in Exercise A. Use words from the word bank for help. Use adverbs of frequency in each sentence.

WEEKDAY ACTIVITIES WORD BANK		
brush my teeth	get ready for bed	make the bed
check my e-mail	get up/wake up	put on makeup
do homework	go to bed	read the newspaper
do the dishes	go to school/work	shave
get dressed	make (eat/have) breakfast/lunch/dinner	take a shower/bath

1. _____

2. _____

3. _____

4. _____

5. _____

6. _____

B. Write a paragraph about a typical day in your life. Use your sentences from Exercise A. Use at least three frequency adverbs in your paragraph. Add a concluding sentence. Write a title for your paragraph.

_____

  During the week, my days are very _____ (busy/boring/interesting).

_____

_____

_____

_____

_____

_____

_____

Revising

A. Exchange paragraphs with a partner. Read the paragraph your partner wrote. Then use the Revising Checklist to help your partner improve his or her paragraph.

REVISING CHECKLIST		
	YES	**NO**
1. Is the title written correctly?		
2. Does each sentence begin with a capital letter and end with correct punctuation?		
3. Does the paragraph have a concluding sentence?		
4. Are the sentences in correct time order?		
5. Are there at least three adverbs of frequency?		
6. Are prepositions of time used correctly?		

B. Use your partner's suggestions to revise your paragraph on a separate piece of paper. Put it in your portfolio.

WRITING ABOUT SPECIAL DAYS

Not all days are typical. Some days are special. Think about special days in your life and holidays in your culture.

A. Discuss these questions in small groups.

1. How do you celebrate birthdays in your culture?

2. What are the most important holidays in your country?

3. What is your favorite day of the year? Why?

B. **Read the paragraph a student wrote about her favorite holiday.**

My Favorite Holiday

My favorite holiday is Songkran, the traditional Thai New Year. We celebrate Songkran from April 13 to April 15. Most businesses, schools, and banks are closed. Many people who live in big cities go back to their hometowns for three days to celebrate with their family and friends. At the beginning of Songkran, we clean our houses. We also cook traditional Thai food such as pad Thai for our family and friends. We usually wear new clothes and go to the temple to pray and give food to the monks. Young people sprinkle water on their parents' and grandparents' hands to show respect. Then the real fun begins. Everyone goes outdoors. There are parades and beauty contests in the streets. Children and adults stand on the side of the road and throw water on people passing by. In fact, Songkran is famous for splashing water and even water fights. It's very hot, so no one really minds getting wet. All over Thailand, Songkran is a time for fun, family, and getting wet. If you plan to visit Thailand during Songkran, make your hotel reservations early. Also leave your camera in your hotel room because it will get wet!

WRITING ABOUT A HOLIDAY

Prewriting

Ask and answer these questions with a partner.

1. What is your favorite holiday?

2. When do you celebrate it?

3. Are businesses open or closed?

4. How do you celebrate this holiday?

5. Who do you celebrate it with?

6. What special foods do you eat?

7. What do you wear?

8. Where do you go to celebrate?

9. Do you give or receive gifts?

10. Why do you like this holiday?

Writing

A. **Write answers to the questions about your favorite holiday in the Prewriting activity. Use complete sentences.**

1. _____

2. _____

3. _____

4. _____

5. _____

6. _____

7. _____

8. _____

9. _____

10. _____

B. **Write a paragraph about your favorite holiday. Use your sentences from Exercise A as a guide. Add any other information that will make your paragraph more interesting. Remember to begin with a topic sentence and include a title.**

_____

_____

_____

_____

_____

_____

_____

_____

_____

_____

_____

_____

Revising

A. Exchange paragraphs with a partner. Read the paragraph your partner wrote. Then use the Revising Checklist to help your partner improve his or her paragraph.

REVISING CHECKLIST	YES	NO
1. Is the first word of the paragraph indented?		
2. Does each sentence begin with a capital letter and end with correct punctuation?		
3. Does the paragraph have a topic sentence?		
4. Is there a title?		
5. Are all of the sentences about the main idea?		

B. Use your partner's suggestions to revise your paragraph on a separate piece of paper. Put it in your portfolio.

YOU BE THE EDITOR

The paragraph below has five mistakes with prepositions of time. With a partner, find and correct the mistakes.

A Busy Pharmacist and Mother

I am a pharmacist and a mother, and my days are busy. As a pharmacist, my job is to prepare and sell medicines. Every morning, I get up on 6:30 A.M. I have breakfast with my family and make lunch for my daughter to take to school. I leave the house at 8:00 A.M. and drive to the drugstore where I work for 9:00 A.M. at 5:00 P.M. During the day, I fill prescriptions for customers. Sometimes the customers have questions about their medicines. I answer their questions. I also give them information about how often to take the medicine. After work, I drive home and have dinner with my family. Then I help my daughter with her homework during a few hours. Sometimes I read or watch TV at the evening before I go to bed. I am very busy, but I really enjoy being a pharmacist and a mother.

Writing a Message on a Card

**Do you like to send cards to your friends and family? Look at the fronts of these cards.
Write a two- or three-sentence message on the inside to someone you know.**

Dear Evelyn,

Happy Birthday! I can't believe you're 21! I'm so sorry I won't be there to celebrate with you. I hope you have a great day and a wonderful year.

Love,
Aunt Susan

WRITING DESCRIPTIONS

DESCRIBING PEOPLE

A. **Look at the pictures of people waiting for a train. Match each person to the description. Write the correct letter under each picture.**

1. _____   2. _____   3. _____   4. _____   5. _____

a. Mr. Wilcox is a tall, thin middle-aged man. He is bald and has a black mustache. He wears big glasses. He is wearing a blue jacket and a striped tie. He is carrying a briefcase. He is reading a train schedule.

b. Sally is a slender young woman of average height. She has long, straight blond hair and a beautiful smile. She is wearing a plaid coat and leather boots. She is carrying her laptop in a shoulder bag. She is talking on a cell phone.

c. Dennis is a short young man with a round face and curly red hair. He has big green eyes, freckles, and a dimple in his chin. He is wearing his favorite T-shirt and sweatpants. He is carrying a backpack.

d. Tom is a good-looking teenager. He is average height and weight. He has straight black hair and brown eyes. He is wearing a sweatshirt and corduroy pants. He is also wearing a baseball cap and a new pair of white sneakers. He is listening to an iPod.

e. Juanita is an attractive woman. She has long, wavy brown hair and big beautiful eyes. Today her hair is in a ponytail. She is wearing a grey pantsuit and a black turtleneck. She's also wearing a silver necklace and long earrings.

PHYSICAL CHARACTERISTICS WORD BANK

Hair		Eyes	Build	Face	Age	Height
bald	red	blue	average	beard	in his/her 20s, 30s, 60s	average
black	shiny	brown	heavy	dimple		short
blond	short	dark	medium	freckles	middle-aged	tall
braids	shoulder-length	green	plump	heart-shaped	old	
brown	straight	hazel	slender	mole	teenage	
curly	thick	narrow	small	mustache	young	
dark	thin	oval	stocky	oval		
long	wavy	round	strong	round		
ponytail			thin	square		
				wrinkles		

CLOTHING AND PERSONAL ITEMS WORD BANK

Clothes		Jewelry	Footwear	Accessories	
blazer	suit	bracelet	boots	backpack	hat
dress jeans	sweater	earrings	pumps	baseball cap	purse/handbag
pants	sweatpants	necklace	sandals	belt	scarf
shirt/blouse	sweatshirt	ring	shoes	bracelet	umbrella
shorts	T-shirt		sneakers	coat	watch
skirt	turtleneck		socks	glasses	
	vest			gloves	

B. **Look at the pictures. Write a short description of each person. Use words from the word banks to help you.**

1. _____
   _____
   _____
   _____

2. _____
   _____
   _____
   _____
   _____

GRAMMAR GUIDE: PRESENT PROGRESSIVE

We use the simple present to describe things that are generally true and don't change.

Examples:

Josh **is** tall.   He **has** black hair and brown eyes.

We use the present progressive to describe things that are happening now. We often use it to describe what people are doing or wearing now.

Examples:

Sam **is waiting** for a bus.   He **is wearing** a raincoat and carrying an umbrella.

Forming the Present Progressive

The present progressive is formed using two parts: the verb *be* (in the simple present), and the *-ing* form of a verb.

A. **Study the chart about forming the present progressive.**

STATEMENTS	I **am wearing** a hat. You **are wearing** a coat. He/ She **is wearing** gloves. They/We **are wearing** uniforms.
NEGATIVES	I **am not wearing** a hat. You **are not wearing** a coat. He/ She **is not wearing** gloves. They/We **are not wearing** uniforms.
QUESTIONS	**Are** you **wearing** a new scarf? **Is** he **wearing** boots? What **are** you **wearing**? What **is** she **wearing**?

B. **Study the following spelling rules for adding *-ing* to verbs.**

VERB ENDING	EXAMPLES
One consonant + *e*: drop the **-e** and add **-ing**	gi**ve** ⟶ giving ta**ke** ⟶ taking
Two consonants: add **-ing**	le**nd** ⟶ lending fa**ll** ⟶ falling
One vowel + one consonant: double the last consonant and add **-ing** *Exception:* verbs ending in *w, x,* or *y*	beg**in** ⟶ beginning r**un** ⟶ running *Exception:* show ⟶ showing
Two vowels + one consonant: add **-ing**	sl**eep** ⟶ sleeping w**ear** ⟶ wearing

C. Look at the descriptions of the people in Exercise A on page 73. Underline the present progressive verbs in each description.

D. Look at the people in the picture below. What are they doing? What are they wearing? Discuss the picture in small groups. Then write five sentences about the picture using the present progressive.

1. _The woman is wearing a long-sleeved sweater and a long plaid skirt._

2. _____

3. _____

4. _____

5. _____

E. **Have a fashion show. Work with a partner. Make a list of the clothes and accessories your partner is wearing. Use the words from the Clothing and Personal Items Word Bank on page 74 to help you. Ask your teacher for help with any other vocabulary.**

_____

_____

_____

_____

_____

F. **Pretend your partner is a model in a fashion show and you are the announcer. Write sentences that describe what your partner is wearing.**

1. _____

2. _____

3. _____

4. _____

5. _____

6. _____

G. **Choose another classmate to describe. Write a paragraph that describes what the person looks like and what he or she is wearing.**

_____

_____

_____

_____

_____

_____

_____

GRAMMAR GUIDE: ADJECTIVES

An adjective is a word that describes a noun. When you write descriptions, you should use adjectives.

Example:

She has **long black** hair.

In the example sentence, the words *long* and *black* are adjectives that describe the noun *hair*. They answer the question, "What kind of hair?"

A. **Read the rules about using adjectives in English.**

RULE	EXAMPLES
Adjectives have the same form whether they describe singular or plural nouns.	ADJECTIVE ⌐ ⌐ SINGULAR NOUN She is wearing a **new** jacket. ADJECTIVE ⌐ ⌐ PLURAL NOUN They are wearing **new** jackets.
Adjectives come before nouns.	He has **brown** eyes. They are wearing **old** sneakers.
Adjectives can come after the verb **be**.	His eyes are **brown**. Their sneakers are **old**.

B. **Underline the adjectives in the descriptions in Exercise A on page 73.**

C. **Read what a student wrote to describe her appearance. Underline the adjectives.**

My name is Jenny Marsh. I am tall and thin. I have long black hair and big brown eyes. I wear round glasses. Today I am wearing old wool pants and a soft yellow sweater. I have on a brown belt and white sneakers.

DESCRIBING YOURSELF

Prewriting

A. **Attach a photo of yourself. Think about words we use to describe ourselves.**

B. **Answer these questions about yourself.**

1. What color eyes do you have? _____

2. What color hair do you have? _____

3. What length is your hair? _____

4. Are you tall, short, or average height? _____

5. What are you wearing? _____

6. What else are you wearing? _____

7. What kind of shoes are you wearing? _____

Writing

A. **Use the answers to the Prewriting questions to write a description of yourself on a separate piece of paper. Use at least five adjectives. Do not put your name on the paper. Fold your paper in half and give it to your teacher. Your teacher will give your paper to another student who will try to guess who wrote the description.**

B. **When the student returns your description to you, copy it onto the lines. Add a topic sentence.**

My name is _____

_____

_____

_____

_____

_____

_____

_____

Revising

A. **Exchange paragraphs with a partner. Read the paragraph your partner wrote. Then use the Revising Checklist to help your partner improve his or her paragraph.**

REVISING CHECKLIST		
	YES	**NO**
1. Is the first word of the paragraph indented?		
2. Does each sentence begin with a capital letter and end with correct punctuation?		
3. Does the paragraph have a topic sentence?		
4. Are there at least five adjectives to support the topic?		

B. **Use your partner's suggestions to revise your paragraph on a separate piece of paper. Give it the title "What I Look Like" and put it in your portfolio.**

DESCRIBING A PERSON'S CHARACTER

Read the paragraph that a student wrote about her roommate. Then discuss the questions that follow with a partner.

An Organized Roommate

My roommate Akiko is a very organized person. First of all, she keeps her closet very neat. For example, all of her clothes are arranged by color, and her shoes are neatly arranged on the shelf. She also organizes her bookcase. Her books are arranged by topic. She keeps her CDs in her bookcase in alphabetical order so they are always easy to find. Finally, her desk is very organized. She puts all of her important papers in a file in the top drawer so nothing ever gets lost. The top of her desk is always neat, too. Sometimes I laugh at her because she is so organized. However, she never loses anything, and I am always looking for something.

1. What is the main idea of the paragraph?

2. What examples support the main idea?

PARAGRAPH POINTER: Examples

Remember that all paragraphs need sentences that support the topic sentence. A good way to support a topic sentence is to give examples. Use *For instance* or *For example* when you give an example.

Complete the sentences with examples.

1. My friend is very serious. For example, _____

   _____

2. My mother is the kindest person I know. For instance, _____

   _____

3. My neighbor gets angry very easily. For example, _____

   _____

4. My younger brother is really funny. For instance, _____

   _____

Prewriting

Think of a person you know well such as a friend, relative, neighbor, classmate, or teacher. Circle some adjectives from the word bank that describe the person.

ADJECTIVE WORD BANK					
ambitious	dependable	hardworking	messy	quiet	shy
artistic	energetic	helpful	neat	responsible	social
boring	enthusiastic	honest	optimistic	selfish	studious
brave	friendly	jealous	organized	sensitive	talkative
competitive	funny	kind	patient	serious	thrifty
creative	generous	lazy			

Make a Cluster Diagram

Clustering is one way to help you think of ideas to write about. It can help you see how your ideas are connected. In a cluster diagram, you use circles and lines.

A. Look at the sample of clustering a student did before she wrote "An Organized Roommate."

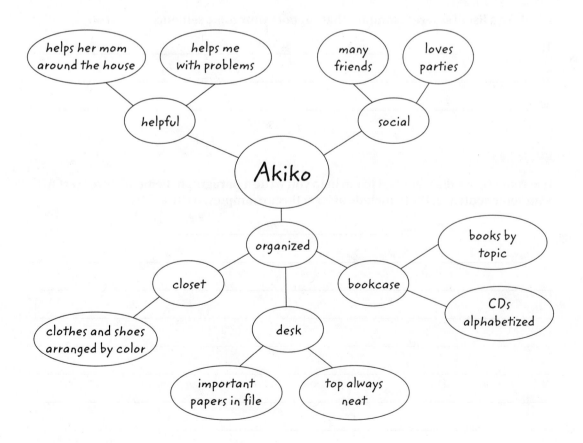

B. Now make your own cluster diagram about the person you chose. Write the person's name in the oval. After you make your cluster diagram, you can see which ideas you want to include in your paragraph.

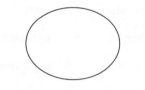

C. Write a topic sentence for a paragraph about the person. Include the name of the person and an adjective from your cluster diagram.

Topic sentence: _____

D. Make a list of several examples that support your topic sentence.

1. _____

2. _____

3. _____

Writing

Use your cluster diagram and list to help you write a paragraph. Remember to start with your topic sentence. Try to include at least three examples. Write a title.

_____

_____

_____

_____

_____

_____

_____

_____

Revising

A. Exchange paragraphs with a partner. Read the paragraph your partner wrote. Then use the Revising Checklist to help your partner improve his or her paragraph.

REVISING CHECKLIST		
	YES	NO
1. Does the paragraph have a topic sentence?		
2. Does the topic sentence give the name of the person and an adjective that describes him or her?		
3. Are there at least three examples to support the topic?		
4. Is there a title?		

B. Use your partner's suggestions to revise your paragraph on a separate piece of paper. Put it in your portfolio.

ON YOUR OWN

Choose one of the following topics and write a paragraph on a separate piece of paper. Give your paragraph a title and put it in your portfolio.

* Write a paragraph about your own character. Give at least three examples to support your topic sentence. Use the title "More about Me."
* Look at the photograph of Ian. Write a description of him. Write about what he looks like. Include what he is wearing and what he is doing.
* Bring one of your favorite photographs or pictures to class. It can be of someone you know or someone in a magazine. Write a description of the person and share it with your classmates.

DESCRIBING THINGS

A. Look at the products featured on the Global Gifts website with a partner. Match the name of the item with the correct picture. Write the name of the item on the line.

candlesticks   flowered plate   Turkish towels

Chinese rug   leather gloves

B. Read the description of each item. Circle the adjectives.

1. This set of two wooden candlesticks was hand-carved in India. It is a perfect addition to your dining-room table. Each 15-inch candlestick was made from one piece of beautiful Indian rosewood. You can order the set for only $65. (Item 001)

2. This 12-inch round plate was hand-painted in Mexico. The colorful design has pictures of flowers, trees, birds, and fish. The bright colors look nice in any room. It is only $30, so order it right away. (Item 002)

3. This rectangular silk and wool rug was made by hand in China. It is 3 feet wide and 6 feet long. The geometric pattern is based on the Chinese symbol for happiness. You can own this beautiful rug for a special price of $530. (Item 003)

4. These plush towels are made of 100% Turkish cotton. You will feel like you're in a spa when you use them. They are so large and soft you can use them at home or at the beach. You can order blue and white stripes or green and white stripes. $20 each. (Item 004)

5. These brown leather gloves are made in Brazil and will keep your hands warm in winter. The leather is soft and smooth. You can order a pair of these attractive gloves in size small, medium, or large. Buy them for yourself, or give them as a gift for $25. (Item 005)

PARAGRAPH POINTER: Details

The key to writing a good description is using specific details. When you describe what someone or something looks like, use lots of details in the supporting sentences so your readers can form a picture in their minds.

Work in small groups. Add specific details for each of the following statements.

1. Our hotel room is awful.
   a. _It smells like cigarette smoke._
   b. _The bed is uncomfortable._
   c. _The clock and lamp don't work._
   d. _It is very small—only 18 feet by 20 feet._
   e. _The window doesn't open._

2. My friend has a nice house.
   a. _____
   b. _____
   c. _____
   d. _____
   e. _____

3. His room is messy.
   a. _____
   b. _____
   c. _____
   d. _____
   e. _____

4. The restaurant is very busy.

a. _____

b. _____

c. _____

d. _____

e. _____

5. The building is old and needs repairs.

a. _____

b. _____

c. _____

d. _____

e. _____

DESCRIBING A PRODUCT FROM YOUR COUNTRY

Prewriting

Find a picture in a magazine or draw a picture of a product from your country. Make a list of words and phrases that describe the product. Use words from the word bank to help you.

_____

_____

_____

_____

_____

DESCRIPTIVE ADJECTIVE WORD BANK				
Opinion	**Shape**	**Texture**	**Design**	**Material**
attractive	circular	bumpy	flowered	cotton
beautiful	oval	furry	geometric	gold
bright	rectangular	fuzzy	plaid	leather
interesting	square	rough	plain	plastic
pretty	triangular	smooth	polka-dotted	silk
		soft	solid	silver
			striped	wood
				wool

Writing

You are listing your product on the Global Gifts website. Use your Prewriting list to write your product description. Begin the description with a sentence that names the product and tells the country it is from. Use at least five adjectives. Include the price of your product.

_____

_____

_____

_____

_____

_____

Revising

A. Exchange descriptions and pictures with a partner. Read the description your partner wrote. Then use the Revising Checklist to help your partner improve his or her description.

REVISING CHECKLIST	YES	NO
1. Is the name of the product and the country it is from stated in the first sentence?		
2. Does the description match the picture of the product?		
3. Are there enough details to clearly describe the product?		
4. Are there at least five adjectives in the description?		
5. Is the price given?		

B. Use your partner's suggestions to revise your description on a separate piece of paper. Put the picture and your description of it in your portfolio.

DESCRIBING A GIFT

Prewriting

A. You are going to write a description of the best or worst gift you have ever received. Think of a gift and make a cluster diagram describing it.

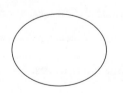

B. **Answer these questions about the gift.**

1. What did you receive? _____

2. What does it look like? _____

3. What is it made of? _____

4. Why do (don't) you like it? _____

C. **Write a topic sentence for a paragraph about the gift.**

Topic sentence: _____

Writing

Use your cluster diagram and the answers to the questions to help you write a description of the gift. Remember to start with your topic sentence. Include details and adjectives. Write a title.

_____

_____

_____

_____

_____

_____

_____

_____

_____

_____

Revising

A. **Exchange paragraphs with a partner. Read the paragraph your partner wrote. Then use the Revising Checklist to help your partner improve his or her paragraph.**

REVISING CHECKLIST		
	YES	**NO**
1. Does the paragraph have a topic sentence?		
2. Does the topic sentence say what the gift is and why your partner likes (or doesn't like) it?		
3. Are there enough details to describe the gift?		
4. Are the adjectives used correctly?		
5. Is there a title?		

B. **Share your description with your classmates.**

DESCRIBING A CAR

Prewriting

A. Look at the pictures of the exterior and interior of a car. With a partner, talk about the parts of a car, using words from the word bank.

CAR WORD BANK				
accelerator	clutch	headlight	roof	taillight
airbag	convertible	hood	seat	tire
blinker	dashboard	horn	seatbelt	trunk
brake	emergency brake	hubcap	side mirror	turn signal
bucket seat	gas tank	hybrid	speedometer	wheel
bumper	gear	license plate	steering wheel	windshield
CD player/radio	GPS	rearview mirror	sunroof	windshield wiper

B. Talk to a partner. Describe a car you own, a car you like, or your dream car. Ask and answer these questions.

1. What color is the car?
2. How many doors does it have?
3. What shape and style is it? Is it a hatchback, an SUV, a station wagon, a sports model, a minivan, or a sedan?
4. What kind of seats does it have?
5. How old is it?
6. Does it have a sunroof?

Writing

A. Write five sentences that describe your car.

1. _____

2. _____

3. _____

4. _____

5. _____

B. Write a paragraph describing your car. Begin with a topic sentence. Include details such as color, size, and style. Use at least four adjectives. Add a title.

_____

_____

_____

_____

_____

_____

_____

_____

Revising

A. Exchange descriptions with a partner and make suggestions for improvement. Then use the Revising Checklist to help your partner further improve his or her description.

REVISING CHECKLIST		
	YES	**NO**
1. Does the paragraph have a topic sentence?		
2. Does the description include details, such as color, size, and style?		
3. Are there enough details to clearly describe the car?		
4. Are there at least four adjectives in the paragraph?		
5. Is there a title?		

B. Write the revised paragraph on a separate piece of paper and put it in your portfolio.

ON YOUR OWN

Choose one of the following topics and write a paragraph on a separate piece of paper. Give your paragraph a title and put it in your portfolio.

- Draw a picture of your national flag. Write about what your flag looks like. Include the colors, shapes, and design. If any of these things have a special meaning, you can write about that, too.
- Describe a piece of sports equipment such as a tennis racquet, a baseball bat, or a ping-pong paddle.
- Write a description of something that you use every day. For example, you can write about your cell phone, toothbrush, or watch.
- What is your favorite painting or piece of art? Describe what it looks like.
- Write a description of your ideal neighbor or roommate.
- Write a description of a character from a movie, TV program, or book.

YOU BE THE EDITOR

The paragraph below has five mistakes with adjectives. With a partner, find and correct the mistakes.

A Birthday Gift

My brother's birthday is next week, and I want to buy him a news sweater. I saw one on the Internet that is made in Canada. I think he will like it. It's a striped sweater blue. My brother has eyes blue, so it will look nice on him. The sweater is made of soft wool, so it is warms. It fits loosely, so it comfortable is to wear. He can wear it to work or on weekends. I'm so happy I had this idea, and I think my brother will be happy, too!

Filling Out an Order Form

You want to order something from Global Gifts on page 84. Complete this order form.

Global Gifts
INTERNATIONAL

**ORDER TOLL-FREE
1-555-555-5555**

Send to: _____

Address: _____

_____

City: _____

State: _____ Zip: _____

Country: _____

Item Number	Quantity	Item Description	Color	Gift Wrap	Price	Total Price
				Yes/No		
Payment Method						
☐ Check		☐ Credit Card			Shipping Charge	$6.00
Card Account Number			Expiration date ___ / ___ Month Year		TOTAL	

Signature _____

Lost-and-Found Messages

Read the Lost-and-Found messages. Then write your own lost or found message.

LOST AND FOUND

Lost
Our adorable black, brown, and white beagle—lost near the park. He is 15 inches tall and weighs 22 pounds. His name is Freckles. If you see him, please call 555-2421.

Lost
Gold wedding ring lost on Peterson Street. I have had it for 30 years, and it is very important to me. If you find it, please call Gabriela at 555-5891.

Found
I found a beautiful, hand-knit red scarf in the cafeteria. E-mail me at DB@school.edu if you think it is yours.

LOST AND FOUND

_____

WRITING ABOUT PLACES

DESCRIBING A ROOM

A. **Look at the picture of a student's bedroom. Then underline the adjectives in the paragraph "A Cozy Bedroom."**

A Cozy Bedroom

My bedroom is small and cozy. There are two big windows on the back wall, so my room is usually bright and sunny. On the left wall, I have a wooden desk with three drawers where I do my homework. All of my books are in a bookcase next to the desk. My bed is on the right wall. There is a painting of a bowl of fruit and flowers above my bed. I love the bright colors of the flowers. I also have a large dresser next to my bed. There are several photographs of my family on top of it and a square mirror above it. Finally, there is a green and white oval rug in front of the dresser. I enjoy spending time in my bedroom.

B. **Look at the pictures. They show three dormitory rooms. In small groups, discuss each picture and make a list of the things in each room. Use the word bank to help you.**

ROOM WORD BANK

alarm clock	chair	ice skates	plant
bedspread	closet	lamp	poster
blinds	computer	laundry basket	rug
bookcase	curtains	mirror	stereo
books	desk	mp3 player	tennis racquet
bulletin board	dresser	nightstand	TV
bunk bed	fan	painting	wastebasket
camera	hockey stick		

Room 1

_____

_____

_____

_____

_____

_____

_____

_____

_____

Room 2

_____

_____

_____

_____

_____

_____

_____

_____

_____

Room 3

_____

_____

_____

_____

_____

_____

_____

_____

_____

C. **What adjectives would you use to describe each room? Use the word bank to help you. Try to add some other words.**

ADJECTIVE WORD BANK				
clean	comfortable	large	neat	small
cluttered	cozy	messy	orderly	sunny

Room 1	Room 2	Room 3
messy		

GRAMMAR GUIDE: _THERE IS_ AND _THERE ARE_

There is and _There are_ are very common phrases in English. We use these phrases at the beginning of a sentence to say that something exists in a specific place. The subject comes after the verb _be_.

Examples:

There is a big window in the classroom.   **There are** lots of windows in the classroom.

There is one computer in my office.   **There are** many computers in the library.

A. **Study the rules below.**

RULE	EXAMPLE
Use **_There is_** with singular noun subjects.	**There is** _a dictionary_ on the table.
Use **_There are_** with plural noun subjects.	**There are** _some books_ on the table.

B. Underline the sentences with *There is* and *There are* in the paragraph "A Cozy Bedroom" on page 93.

C. Work with a partner. Write three sentences beginning with *There is* or *There are* for each room on pages 94–95.

Room 1

1. _____

2. _____

3. _____

Room 2

1. _____

2. _____

3. _____

Room 3

1. _____

2. _____

3. _____

GRAMMAR GUIDE: PREPOSITIONS OF PLACE

When you want to explain where something is located, you need to use correct prepositions. The prepositions in the word bank will help you describe where items are located in relation to other items.

A. **Study the word bank below.**

PREPOSITIONS OF PLACE WORD BANK				
above	beside	in	in front of	on
behind	between	in back of	next to	under

B. **Look at the pictures of rooms. Then complete the descriptions with the correct words from the word bank.**

1. My living room is my favorite room in my house. The couch is big and comfortable.

    There are three pictures _____ the couch. The coffee table is

    _____ the couch. There are some flowers _____ the

    vase _____ the coffee table. I love to sit and read or watch TV in

    the armchair _____ the couch.

2. I spend a lot of time working in my office. There are lots of books

    _____ the bookcase. The fax machine is _____

    a table _____ the bookcase and the desk. There is a computer

    _____ the desk. The wastebasket is _____ the desk.

C. **Look at the picture of a dining room. Practice using prepositions of place by adding
    items from the list to the picture below. Then compare your picture with a classmate's.**

1. Draw a bowl of fruit in front of the grandmother.
2. Draw a dog under the table.
3. Draw a ball beside the dog.
4. Draw a toy next to the ball.
5. Draw a clock on the wall behind the grandfather.
6. Draw a vase between the candles on the table.
7. Draw a flower in the vase.
8. Draw a cake on the long table behind the mother.
9. Draw a painting on the wall above the long table.

DESCRIBING YOUR CLASSROOM

Prewriting

Look around your classroom. Complete the chart.

YOUR CLASSROOM	
1. What color are the walls?	
2. How many windows are there?	
3. How are the students' desks arranged?	
4. Where does the teacher sit?	
5. Where is the door?	
6. What else is in the room (board, clock, posters, etc.)?	
7. Do you like your classroom? Why or why not?	

Writing

Use the information in the chart to write a paragraph that describes your classroom. Use at least three prepositions of place. Also write at least one sentence with *There is* and one sentence with *There are*. Remember to begin with your topic sentence and include a title.

_____

_____

_____

_____

_____

_____

_____

Revising

A. Exchange paragraphs with a partner. Read the paragraph your partner wrote. Then use the Revising Checklist to help your partner improve his or her paragraph.

REVISING CHECKLIST		
	YES	NO
1. Does the paragraph begin with a topic sentence?		
2. Does the paragraph have enough details about the classroom?		
3. Does the paragraph include sentences with *There is* and *There are*?		
4. Are there at least three prepositions of place?		

B. Use your partner's suggestions to revise your paragraph on a separate piece of paper. Put it in your portfolio.

> **PARAGRAPH POINTER:** Space Order
>
> When you write a paragraph that describes a place, you can arrange the details according to where things are located. This is called space order. Use prepositions of place to make the description clear to the reader.

DESCRIBING YOUR FAVORITE ROOM

Prewriting

A. What is your favorite room? Where is it? Draw a simple picture of your room and describe it to a partner.

B. Make a list of the things in your room.

_____   _____

_____   _____

_____   _____

_____   _____

Writing

A. Answer these questions about your favorite room.

1. What size is the room?

   _____

2. What adjectives would you use to describe it?

   _____

3. What pieces of furniture do you have in your room?

   _____

4. What else is there in your room?

   _____

5. Are there any windows? Is it sunny or dark?

   _____

6. What color are the walls?

   _____

7. Why do you like this room?

   _____

B. Complete this sentence for your topic sentence.

My favorite room in my _____ is _____

C. Use the sentences to write a paragraph that describes your room. Use at least three prepositions of place. Also write at least one sentence with *There is* and one sentence with *There are*. Remember to begin with your topic sentence and include a title.

_____

_____

_____

_____

_____

_____

_____

_____

_____

Revising

A. Exchange paragraphs with a partner. Read the paragraph your partner wrote. Then use the Revising Checklist to help your partner improve his or her paragraph.

REVISING CHECKLIST	YES	NO
1. Does the paragraph begin with a topic sentence?		
2. Does the paragraph have enough details?		
3. Does the paragraph include sentences with *There is* and *There are*?		
4. Are there at least three prepositions of place?		

B. Use your partner's suggestions to revise your paragraph on a separate piece of paper. Put it in your portfolio.

WRITING PERSONAL LETTERS

A personal letter is a letter you write to a friend or relative. Personal letters are informal and often written by hand. There are five main parts to a personal letter. Look at the parts labeled on the letter that a student wrote to her mother.

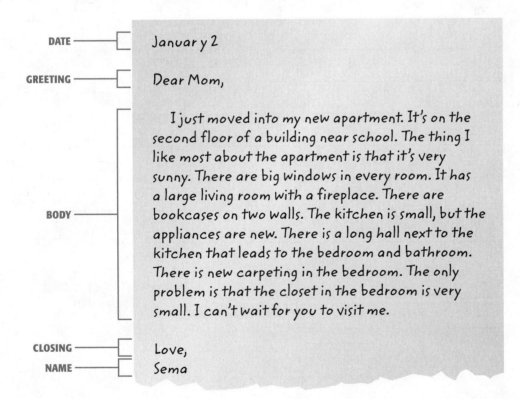

DATE — January 2

GREETING — Dear Mom,

BODY —
I just moved into my new apartment. It's on the second floor of a building near school. The thing I like most about the apartment is that it's very sunny. There are big windows in every room. It has a large living room with a fireplace. There are bookcases on two walls. The kitchen is small, but the appliances are new. There is a long hall next to the kitchen that leads to the bedroom and bathroom. There is new carpeting in the bedroom. The only problem is that the closet in the bedroom is very small. I can't wait for you to visit me.

CLOSING — Love,
NAME — Sema

- Use a comma after the greeting: *Dear _____, Hi _____,* etc.
- Use a comma after the closing: *Love, Best, Best wishes, Take care,* etc.

DESCRIBING WHERE YOU LIVE

Prewriting

Think about the place where you live. Describe your house or apartment to a partner. Discuss the things you like and don't like about the place. Ask and answer these questions:

1. Where do you live?
2. How big is your home? How many rooms does it have? What size are the rooms?
3. Is your home old or new?
4. Is it sunny or dark? Are there lots of windows?
5. Do you like your home? Why or why not?

Writing

Write a letter to a friend or relative that describes your home. Use the letter on page 101 as a guide.

_____ (date)

Dear _____ ,

_____

_____

_____

_____

_____

_____

_____

Love,

_____

Revising

After your teacher has read your letter and given suggestions, revise your letter on a separate piece of paper. Put it in your portfolio.

WRITING TO A FRIEND

Prewriting

You are going to write a letter to a friend who is coming to visit you. Make a cluster diagram of the places to go and things to do in the city where you live. Put the name of your city or town in the center circle.

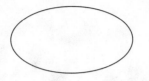

Writing

Use your cluster diagram to complete the letter.

_____ (date)

Dear _____ ,

    I was so happy when you called to tell me you were coming

to _____ to visit me. There are lots of places to go

and things to see and do here. We can _____

_____

_____

_____

_____

Love,

_____

Revising

Exchange your letter with a partner. Use your partner's suggestions to revise your letter on a separate piece of paper. Put it in your portfolio.

Prewriting

A. Look at the famous photograph called *Lunchtime atop a Skyscraper*, taken by
Charles C. Ebbets in 1932. It shows New York City construction workers eating lunch.

B. Write four sentences that describe the photograph. Use the present progressive and
prepositions of place.

1. _____

2. _____

3. _____

4. _____

Writing

Use the sentences you wrote to write a descriptive paragraph about the picture.

_____

_____

_____

_____

_____

Revising

Exchange descriptive paragraphs with a partner. Read the paragraph your partner
wrote. Make suggestions for improvement. Use your partner's suggestions to revise your
paragraph on a separate piece of paper. Put it in your portfolio.

USE YOUR IMAGINATION

You have just moved into a new apartment. This is the living room. It is very simple and plain. The walls are white and there are no decorations.

Prewriting

A. **Talk to a partner. Use your imagination to describe how you would improve this room. Your landlord is going to pay for everything, so don't worry about money!**

B. **What things would you add to this living room? Draw them in the picture.**

C. **Make a list of the furniture and other items in the room.**

_____   _____

_____   _____

_____   _____

Writing

Write a description of the room.

_____

_____

_____

_____

_____

_____

_____

Revising

Exchange descriptions with a partner. Read the description your partner wrote. Make suggestions for improvement. Use your partner's suggestions to revise your description on a separate piece of paper. Put it in your portfolio.

ON YOUR OWN

Choose one of the following topics. When you are done with your first draft, revise and edit your paragraph.

- Write a description of an unusual room.
- Write a paragraph describing the nicest or worst hotel room you have stayed in.
- What is your favorite restaurant? Describe what it looks like in a paragraph.
- Write a description of a bus or taxi in your city. What does it look like on the outside? What does it look like on the inside?
- What does your locker at school look like? Is it messy or neat? Write a description of it.
- Write a paragraph describing the closet where you keep your clothes and shoes. How big is it? Does it have any shelves? Is it messy or neat?
- Write a paragraph describing a park in your city or town.

YOU BE THE EDITOR

Read the paragraph. It has seven mistakes with prepositions of place and with *There is* and *There are*. With a partner, find and correct the mistakes.

A Messy Bedroom

My son's bedroom is a mess. He didn't make his bed or hang up his clothes. There is dirty clothes in the floor. I even found dirty clothes between his bed. His schoolbooks and papers are all over his desk. There are an empty soda can of his night table. The top of his dresser is covered with newspapers and magazines. There are a wet towel on the chair instead of at the laundry basket. I wish he would clean up his room!

Addressing an Envelope

A. **Look at the sample envelope.**

Toby Boxer
52 Walden Street
Ames, IA 50010

Ms. Charlotte Brown
234 Benefit Street
Providence, RI 02912

B. **Address the envelope for the letter you wrote to your friend on page 103. Put your name and address in the upper left-hand corner. Then put the person's name and address in the middle.**

WRITING A NARRATIVE

WRITING A STORY

A. **Read the story.**

A Frightening Experience

Last week I had a frightening experience on an elevator. I was on my way to have dinner at my friend's apartment. I got on the elevator in the lobby and pushed the button for the fifth floor. The elevator stopped at the third floor and a couple got on with their baby. The woman pushed the button for the eighth floor, the doors closed, and the elevator started to go up. A few seconds later, the elevator stopped suddenly. Then I felt the elevator bounce up and down two times. We all looked at each other, and the baby began to cry. I was very nervous. A few minutes later the elevator door opened. We were stuck between the third and fourth floors. The third floor was about five feet down. Luckily, I had my cell phone with me, and I called my friend. We waited in the elevator for about ten minutes, but it felt like ten hours. Finally, my friend brought a ladder to the third floor, and we all climbed out of the elevator safely. I was happy to be out of the elevator, but my stomach hurt and I couldn't eat dinner.

B. **Number the pictures so they tell the story in the correct time order.**

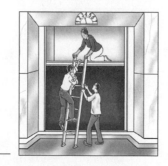

GRAMMAR GUIDE: SIMPLE PAST

We use the simple past to write about an event that started and finished in the past. Many English verbs are regular and form the simple past by adding -ed to the base form. To write a negative sentence in the simple past, add *did not/didn't* before the verb.

A. **Study the chart that shows how to form sentences and questions for most verbs in the simple past.**

STATEMENTS	I **played** basketball yesterday. You **helped** your brother. He/She **worked** late. They/We **watched** TV.
NEGATIVES	I **didn't drive** to school. You **didn't go** to the movies. He/She **didn't bring** his/her books. They/We **didn't watch** the game.
QUESTIONS	**Did** you **see** the movie? **Did** he/she **call** you? **What did** you **wear**? **What did** he/she **read**?

B. **Study the following spelling rules for forming the simple past of regular verbs.**

VERB ENDING	EXAMPLES
One vowel + *y*: add **-ed** Two consonants: add **-ed** Two vowels + one consonant: add **-ed**	enjoy ⟶ enjoy**ed** walk ⟶ walk**ed** need ⟶ need**ed**
One consonant + *e*: add **-d**	arrive ⟶ arrive**d**
One consonant + *y*: change the **y** to **i** and add **-ed**	study ⟶ stud**ied**
One vowel + one consonant: double the final consonant and add **-ed**	plan ⟶ plan**ned**

The verb *be* forms the simple past in a different way.

C. **Study the chart below.**

STATEMENTS	I **was** late for class. You **were** late for class. He/She **was** late for class.	We **were** late for class. You **were** late for class. They **were** late for class.
NEGATIVES	I **was not (wasn't)** late for class. He/She **was not (wasn't)** late for class.	You **were not (weren't)** late for class. They **were not (weren't)** late for class.
QUESTIONS	**Was** she late for class? **Were** they late for class? **Why** was she late for class?	

D. There are also many common irregular verbs in English. Study the chart.

SIMPLE PAST OF COMMON IRREGULAR VERBS			
Base Form	**Past Form**	**Base Form**	**Past Form**
beat	beat	have	had
become	became	leave	left
begin	began	make	made
bring	brought	say	said
build	built	see	saw
come	came	sell	sold
drive	drove	speak	spoke
fall	fell	spend	spent
find	found	take	took
fly	flew	teach	taught
get	got	tell	told
give	gave	think	thought
go	went	wake	woke

E. Underline the simple past verbs in "A Frightening Experience" on page 108.

F. Rewrite the paragraph below in the simple past.

I have a busy day. I wake up at 7:00 A.M. and get dressed. Then, I eat breakfast, read the paper, and check my e-mail. After that, I take the bus to school and go to classes from 10:00 A.M. to 4:00 P.M. Next, I study for a few hours at the library before I have a quick dinner and go to work at the bookstore on campus. At 9:30 P.M., my friend drives me home. When I get home, I watch the news on TV and go to sleep.

I had a busy day yesterday. _____

_____

_____

_____

_____

_____

_____

G. Read the story and fill in the blanks with the correct past form of the verb. Compare your answers with a partner's.

The Google Guys

Sergey Brin and Larry Page _____ (invent) the Internet search engine Google. Sergey was born in Moscow in 1973. His mother and father _____ (be) both mathematicians. Sergey and his family _____ (move) to the United States when he was six. When Sergey was nine years old, his father _____ (give) him his first computer. He _____ (love) it, and from then on, his interest in computers _____ (continue) to grow. Sergey _____ (graduate) from the University of Maryland in 1993. After that, he _____ (go) to graduate school at Stanford University.

Larry Page was born in 1973 in Michigan. His father _____ (be) a professor of computer science, and his mother _____ (teach) computer programming. Like Sergey, Larry _____ (love) computers at an early age. Larry _____ (study) computer engineering at the University of Michigan. He _____ (earn) his B.S.E. in 1995 and then _____ (go) on to graduate school at Stanford University.

Sergey and Larry _____ (meet) at Stanford and _____ (become) friends. They _____ (write) a paper together and _____ (create) their own search engine _____ (call) BackRub. BackRub _____ (grow), and in 1998 it _____ (become) Google.

Google _____ (be) an immediate success. Soon people all over the world _____ (start) using Google as their search engine. In fact, Google _____ (make) both men billionaires.

WRITING NARRATIVE PARAGRAPHS

Activity 1

A. Work with a partner. Look at the four pictures. They tell a story about a couple who had a bad experience at a restaurant. The pictures are not in the correct order. Number the pictures so they tell the story in a logical order.

_____

_____

_____

_____

B. Write a sentence or two for each picture. Tell what happened. Use the simple past.

Picture 1: _____

_____

Picture 2: _____

_____

Picture 3: _____

_____

Picture 4: _____

_____

C. Take turns telling the story to your partner. Use your sentences.

Activity 2

Each group of sentences tells a story, but the sentences are not in the correct time order. Number the sentences so they follow a logical order. Then write the sentences in paragraph form.

1.

_____ My sister called an ambulance, and it took me to the hospital.

_____ On the first day I was there, I fell down on an icy sidewalk and broke my ankle.

_____ For the rest of my trip, I had to use crutches to get around.

_1_ Last month I went to Chicago to visit my sister.

_____ After that, I spent five hours at Chicago General Hospital.

My Trip to Chicago

_____

_____

_____

_____

_____

_____

_____

2.

_____ By lunchtime it was warmer, so I took the sweater off in the cafeteria.

_____ When I told Ellen, she was furious because her boyfriend's mother had made it.

_____ Yesterday my roommate, Ellen, got very mad at me.

_____ It was cold in the morning, and I borrowed a sweater from her.

_____ After lunch, I forgot about the sweater and left it in the cafeteria.

_____ In fact, Ellen was so angry that she didn't speak to me for the rest of the day.

_____ Later, I went back to get it, but the sweater was gone!

_____

_____

_____

_____

_____

_____

_____

3.

_____ I left school feeling sad because everyone I knew forgot my birthday.

_____ One of my best birthdays was the day I turned eighteen.

_____ Then, I went to school expecting birthday wishes from all of my friends, but not one of my friends or teachers wished me a happy birthday.

_____ I woke up early in a good mood, but when I sat down for breakfast with my family, no one wished me a happy birthday.

_____ It was the best birthday party I ever had.

_____ As soon as I walked in the door, everyone yelled "Surprise! Happy Birthday."

_____ On the way home from school, I noticed that there were a lot of cars parked outside my house, and all the lights were turned off.

_____ I was surprised to see all of my friends and my whole family standing around a big birthday cake.

A Birthday Surprise

_____

_____

_____

_____

_____

_____

_____

_____

4.

_____ The day started off badly when I woke up an hour late and didn't have time to take a shower or eat breakfast.

_____ When I finally got to the office building, the parking lot was full and I had to park far away from the building.

_____ My first job interview was a terrible experience.

_____ On my way to the interview, I hit heavy traffic.

_____ I had to walk two blocks in the rain without an umbrella.

_____ Obviously, I didn't get the job.

_____ By the time I got to the building, I was an hour late and soaking wet.

_____ When I finally walked into the manager's office, I realized I forgot my résumé.

My Worst Job Interview

_____

_____

_____

_____

_____

_____

_____

_____

_____

_____

_____

PARAGRAPH POINTER: Narrative Paragraphs

A narrative paragraph tells a story about something that happened in the past. When you write a narrative paragraph, use time order to organize your sentences. Also, include time-order signal words.

Prewriting

A. **Complete the sentences so that each one is true for you.**

1. One of the _____ (happiest/saddest/scariest/most embarrassing)

   memories of my childhood happened when I was _____ years old.

2. A very _____ (funny/embarrassing/surprising) thing happened to me on

   my first day of _____.

3. One summer my friends and I had a(n) _____ experience.

4. My trip to _____ was very _____.

5. One of the most enjoyable (days/evenings/weeks/weekends) I ever spent was

   _____.

B. **Discuss the experiences in groups. Tell what happened in each situation.**

C. **Choose an experience from Exercise A to write about. List the events you want to include in your story. Number them in the correct time order.**

Writing

Write a story about the experience you chose. Use the sentence from Exercise A as your topic sentence. Be sure to use the simple past and time-order signal words. Give your story a title.

_____

_____

_____

_____

_____

_____

_____

_____

Revising

A. Exchange paragraphs with a partner. Read the paragraph your partner wrote. Then use the Revising Checklist to help your partner improve his or her paragraph.

REVISING CHECKLIST	YES	NO
1. Is there a topic sentence?		
2. Are the sentences in the correct time order?		
3. Are the simple past verbs in the correct form?		
4. Does the paragraph include time-order signal words?		

B. Use your partner's suggestions to revise your story on a separate piece of paper. Share it with your classmates and put it in your portfolio.

USE YOUR IMAGINATION

A. Look at the photo. It shows a traffic jam. Talk about the photo with a partner.

B. Write a story based on the photo. Imagine that you are in one of the cars. Tell your reader the time and place of your story in the first sentence. Tell what happened in the next few sentences. Use the simple past.

_____

_____

_____

_____

_____

_____

_____

C. Exchange stories with another student. Read your partner's story. Give your story the title "A Traffic Jam" and put it in your portfolio.

WRITING A BIOGRAPHY OF NEIL ARMSTRONG

A biography tells the story of a person's life.

Prewriting

A. **Look at the photo of astronaut Neil Armstrong. Discuss what you know about him with a partner.**

B. **Look at the timeline of important events in Neil Armstrong's life. Talk about the important events in Armstrong's life with your partner.**

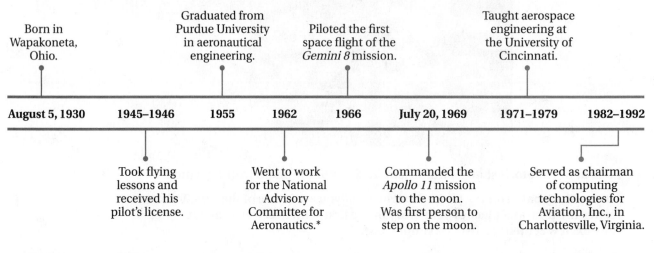

Born in Wapakoneta, Ohio.		Graduated from Purdue University in aeronautical engineering.		Piloted the first space flight of the *Gemini 8* mission.			Taught aerospace engineering at the University of Cincinnati.	
August 5, 1930	**1945–1946**	**1955**	**1962**	**1966**	**July 20, 1969**	**1971–1979**	**1982–1992**
	Took flying lessons and received his pilot's license.		Went to work for the National Advisory Committee for Aeronautics.*		Commanded the *Apollo 11* mission to the moon. Was first person to step on the moon.		Served as chairman of computing technologies for Aviation, Inc., in Charlottesville, Virginia.

Writing

A. **Write at least one complete sentence for each fact on the timeline.**

1. _____

2. _____

3. _____

4. _____

5. _____

*a government agency that researched airplanes

6. _____

7. _____

8. _____

B. Look at the sentences you wrote about Neil Armstrong. Add time-order signal words.

C. Use your sentences to complete the paragraph about Neil Armstrong. Be sure to use time-order signal words so that the order of events is clear.

Neil Armstrong is a famous astronaut. _____

_____

_____

_____

_____

_____

_____

_____

_____

Today, Armstrong is retired and lives on his farm in Lebanon, Ohio. _____

Revising

A. Revise your paragraph. Add these two sentences to your paragraph.

Armstrong has flown more than 200 different models of aircraft, including jets, rockets, helicopters, and gliders.

His first words after stepping on the moon were, "That's one small step for a man, one giant leap for mankind."

_____

_____

_____

_____

_____

_____

_____

_____

_____

_____

B. Exchange paragraphs with a partner. Read the paragraph your partner wrote. Then use the Revising Checklist to help your partner improve his or her paragraph.

REVISING CHECKLIST	YES	NO
1. Is there a topic sentence?		
2. Are the sentences in the correct time order?		
3. Are the simple past verbs in the correct form?		
4. Does the paragraph include time-order signal words?		

C. Use your partner's suggestions to revise your paragraph on a separate piece of paper. Share it with your classmates. Then give it the title "Neil Armstrong" and put it in your portfolio.

WRITING A BIOGRAPHY OF CHRISTIANE AMANPOUR

Prewriting

A. Look at the photo of Christiane Amanpour. Have you ever seen her on TV? Discuss what you know about her with a partner.

B. Look at the timeline for Christiane Amanpour. Talk about the important events in Amanpour's life with your partner.

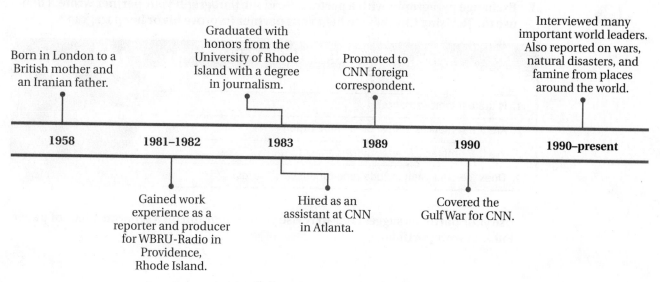

Writing

A. Write at least one sentence for each fact on the timeline. Use a variety of time-order signal words.

1. _____
2. _____
3. _____
4. _____
5. _____
6. _____
7. _____

B. Use your sentences to complete the paragraph about Christiane Amanpour.

Christiane Amanpour is one of the most successful international news
reporters in the world.
_____
_____
_____
_____
_____
_____
_____

Revising

A. **Exchange paragraphs with a partner. Read the paragraph your partner wrote. Then use the Revising Checklist to help your partner improve his or her paragraph.**

REVISING CHECKLIST	YES	NO
1. Is there a topic sentence?		
2. Are the sentences in the correct time order?		
3. Are the simple past verbs in the correct form?		
4. Does the paragraph include time-order signal words?		

B. **Use your partner's suggestions to revise your paragraph on a separate piece of paper. Put it in your portfolio.**

WRITING A BIOGRAPHY OF ICHIRO SUZUKI

Prewriting

A. **Look at the photo of baseball player Ichiro Suzuki. Discuss what you know about him with a partner.**

B. **Look at the timeline for Ichiro Suzuki. Talk about the important events in Suzuki's life with your partner.**

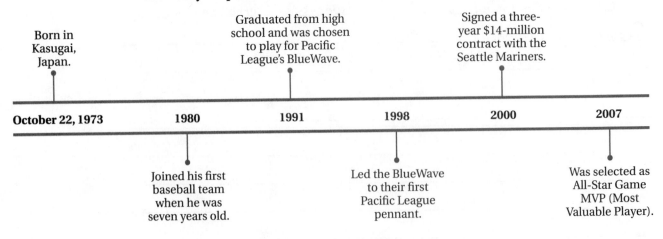

Writing

A. **Write at least one sentence for each fact on the timeline. Use time-order signal words.**

1. _____

2. _____

3. _____

4. _____

5. _____

6. _____

B. **Use your sentences to complete a paragraph about Ichiro Suzuki. Begin with a topic sentence.**

_____

_____

_____

_____

_____

_____

_____

_____

_____

_____

_____

_____

Revising

A. **Exchange paragraphs with a partner. Read the paragraph your partner wrote. Then use the Revising Checklist to help your partner improve his or her paragraph.**

REVISING CHECKLIST		
	YES	**NO**
1. Does the paragraph begin with a topic sentence?		
2. Are the sentences in the correct time order?		
3. Are the simple past verbs in the correct form?		
4. Are there time-order signal words?		

B. **Use your partner's suggestions to revise your paragraph on a separate piece of paper. Give it the title "Ichiro Suzuki" and put it in your portfolio.**

Choose one of the following famous people to write about. Or choose another person and do some research about him or her. Write a paragraph about the person.

A.

Name:	GILBERTO GIL
Place of Birth:	Salvador, Brazil
Date of Birth:	June 29, 1942
Occupation:	Musician, songwriter, environmentalist, and politician

Accomplishments:
- 1987: Served as Secretary of Culture for the city of Salvador
- 1990: Joined Brazil's Green Party and founded Blue Wave, an environmental protection organization to protect Brazil's waters and coastline
- 2003–2008: Served as Brazilian Minister of Culture
- Released more than 40 albums; had 6 gold records and 4 platinum singles; sold 5 million records

Honors:
- 1998: Grammy Award for Best World Music Album for *Quanta Live*
- 2003: Person of the Year, Latin Academy of Recording Arts and Sciences
- 2005: Grammy Award for Best Contemporary World Music Album for *Eletracústico*

B.

Name:	LORENA OCHOA
Place of Birth:	Guadalajara, Mexico
Date of Birth:	November 15, 1981
Occupation:	Professional golfer

Accomplishments:
- Has been ranked number one female golfer in the world
- 2001: Won the Mexico National Sports Award
- 2003: LPGA (Ladies Professional Golf Association) Rookie of the Year
- 2006, 2007: LPGA Player of the Year
- 2006, 2007, 2008: Vare Trophy (scoring leader)
- 2008: Won the Corona Championship in Mexico; qualified for the World Golf Hall of Fame

WRITING YOUR AUTOBIOGRAPHY

Prewriting

A. Make a timeline of the important events in your own life on a separate piece of paper. Describe your timeline to a partner.

B. Write at least one sentence for each event on your timeline.

1. _____

2. _____

3. _____

4. _____

5. _____

6. _____

Writing

Use your sentences to write a paragraph about yourself. Tell where and when you were born in the topic sentence. Use simple past verbs and time-order signal words.

_____

_____

_____

_____

_____

_____

_____

_____

_____

_____

Revising

A. Exchange paragraphs with a partner. Read the paragraph your partner wrote. Then use the Revising Checklist to help your partner improve his or her paragraph.

REVISING CHECKLIST		
	YES	NO
1. Is there a topic sentence?		
2. Are the sentences in the correct time order?		
3. Are the simple past verbs in the correct form?		
4. Are there time-order signal words?		

B. Use your partner's suggestions to revise your paragraph on a separate piece of paper. Give it the title "My Autobiography" and put it in your portfolio with your timeline.

Using Poetry to Write about Memories

Sometimes it is fun to write a poem about a special memory. Here are some examples of simple memory poems:

Lorentza in Monterrey, 4 years old

Sitting in a tree
Waiting for my father to come home from work

Koichi in Tokyo, 11 years old

Playing baseball after school
Eating junk food before dinner

Letizia in Forte dei Marmi, 17 years old

Playing the guitar
Singing with my friends

Abdullah in Jeddah, 8 years old

Riding a donkey
Getting water for my family

A. **To write this type of memory poem, think back to a specific time in your childhood. Think about how old you were, where you were, and what you were doing. Use the examples as a guide.**

1. On the first line, write your first name and the name of the place where you were.

   _____

2. On the next line, write your age at that time.

   _____

3. On the third line, write exactly what you were doing (use the *-ing* form of the verb).

   _____

4. On the last line, give further information about what was happening (use the *-ing* form of the verb).

   _____

5. Make any changes that you want to make in your memory poem. Then copy it on the lines.

   _____

   _____

   _____

   _____

B. **Copy your memory poem onto a separate piece of paper and put it in your portfolio with the title "My Memory Poem."**

Memory Drawing

A. **Think of a special memory from your childhood. Do a very simple drawing of that memory on a separate piece of paper.**

B. **Use the ideas in your drawing to write a paragraph about this memory. Write the revised paragraph under your drawing. When you are finished, give it the title "A Memory from My Childhood." Put the drawing and the paragraph in your portfolio.**

ON YOUR OWN

Choose one of the following topics. When you are done with your first draft, revise and edit your paragraph to improve it.

- Moving to a new place can be a difficult experience. Write a paragraph about a time you moved.
- Write about a time when you tried to do something but failed.
- Write about an experience that changed the direction of your life.
- Did you ever forget something important? Write about that experience.
- Write about a memorable sporting event in your life.
- Do you remember your first day of school? Write a paragraph about that day.

YOU BE THE EDITOR

The paragraph below has six mistakes with simple past verbs. With a partner, find and correct the mistakes.

My First Camping Trip

My first camping trip was not at all what I expected. My brother and I packed our car Friday afternoon and drived five hours to a beautiful campsite in Maine. I thinked it would be hard to put up our tent, but it were easy. It only took a few minutes. We made a fire and cooked a delicious dinner over the fire. We enjoy a beautiful sunset. Then we went into the tent and falled asleep surrounded by the peace and quiet of the trees. There were no bugs and no bears. It rained a little in the night, but we were warm and dry in our tent. When we woked up, the sun was out and we took a walk along the river. What a surprise. I like camping!

REAL-LIFE WRITING

Writing a Postcard

A. Read the postcard. It was sent from a student who visited Rio de Janeiro, Brazil. It shows the correct form for writing and addressing a postcard.

Dear Aya,

Rio de Janeiro is awesome! We spent yesterday on Ipanema Beach. Last night we went to some great clubs. Today we went to Carnival, spelled *Carnaval* in Portuguese. The music, dancing, and costumes were all amazing. Rio is the city that never sleeps, especially during Carnaval! You must visit Rio before you go back to Japan.

See you soon.

Love,
Muriel

Ms. Aya Ochiai

551 West Cedar Street

Ann Arbor, MI 48105

B. Draw a simple picture that shows a place you have visited. Then write a message to a friend or relative about your trip. Address the postcard correctly.

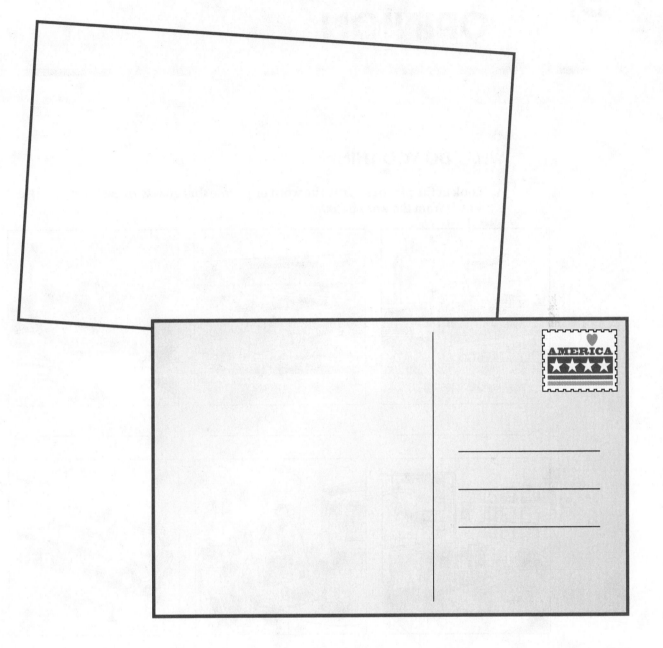

EXPRESSING YOUR OPINION

WHAT DO YOU THINK?

A. **Look at the pictures. Write the word or phrase that goes with each picture. Use words from the word bank.**

1. _____

2. _____

3. _____

4. _____

5. _____

6. _____

7. _____

8. _____

9. _____

10. _____

11. _____

12. _____

B. **A ban is a law that says people cannot do something. Talk to a partner about where you think there should be a ban on smoking. Draw the "No Smoking" sign on the pictures.**

C. **Read the paragraphs and answer the questions that follow.**

1.   I think there should be a ban on smoking in public places. First of all, nonsmokers have a right to clean air. They should not have to be around cigarette smoke. Like most nonsmokers, I hate it when my clothes smell of cigarette smoke. It is disgusting, and it is also dangerous. People can get sick and even die from breathing second-hand smoke. Another reason smoking should be banned in public places is that it is so bad for the health of smokers. Maybe banning it will help smokers quit smoking. If smokers do not quit because of the cost or the health warnings, maybe these new laws will help them quit.

a. What is the author's opinion?

_____

b. What reasons does the author give to support his or her opinion?

_____

_____

_____

_____

2.   It is unfair to ban smoking in public places. For one thing, nonsmokers should not have more rights than smokers. Also, if nonsmokers don't want to be in a smoke-filled room, they can go somewhere else. In addition, smoking is a legal activity. I do not believe that the government should tell people that a legal activity is illegal in some places. Finally, I think banning smoking in places like restaurants is bad for business. Maybe both smokers and nonsmokers should try to be a little more understanding.

a. What is the author's opinion?

_____

b. What reasons does the author give to support his or her opinion?

_____

_____

_____

_____

GRAMMAR GUIDE: *SHOULD*

We often use *should* or *should not* (*shouldn't*) to give an opinion or advice.

A. **Review the examples of sentences that use *should*.**

STATEMENTS	I think you **should** take the English course. He **should** exercise every day. You **should** eat a healthy breakfast. You **should** turn off the lights when you leave a room.
NEGATIVE STATEMENTS	People **shouldn't (should not)** talk on their cell phones in restaurants. We **shouldn't (should not)** drive cars that use a lot of gas. You **shouldn't (should not)** leave the window open.
QUESTIONS	**Should** I e-mail Tom about the meeting? **Should** I take driving classes? **Should** I get a part-time job?

B. Study the rules for using *should*.

RULE	EXAMPLE
Should is always followed by the base form of the verb.	Maria **should** *sign* the lease immediately. (CORRECT) Maria **should** *signed* the lease immediately. (INCORRECT)
Do not add **-s** to **should** even if you are using the third person singular.	My brother **should** *work* harder. (CORRECT) My brother **shoulds** *work* harder. (INCORRECT)
Do not use an infinitive (**to** + base form) after **should**.	You **should** *stop* smoking. (CORRECT) You **should** *to stop* smoking. (INCORRECT)

C. Write two sentences of advice for each situation. Use *should* in one sentence and *shouldn't* in the other sentence.

1. Jason has a toothache.

   a.   *He should go to the dentist.*

   b.   *He shouldn't eat candy.*

2. Marty burned his hand.

   a. _____

   b. _____

3. Emma has a cold.

   a. _____

   b. _____

4. Paula has the hiccups.

   a. _____

   b. _____

5. Stan has a fever.

a. _____

b. _____

6. Julie has a stomachache.

a. _____

b. _____

D. **Compare your sentences with a partner's. Did you give the same advice?**

PARAGRAPH POINTER: Order of Importance

You have learned to organize the supporting sentences in paragraphs according to time and space order. Now you will practice organizing supporting sentences according to order of importance. When you use order of importance, you list your ideas from most important to least important or least important to most important.

Before you write a paragraph that expresses your opinion, you should first make a list of reasons to support your opinion. Then, you should arrange the reasons according to their order of importance. When you write your paragraph, use signal words to help the reader understand your ideas.

A. **Review these signal words.**

SIGNAL WORDS OF ADDITION WORD BANK			
also,	first of all,	in addition,	most importantly,
finally,	for one thing,	last of all,	secondly,

B. **Complete the opinion paragraphs below with words and phrases from the word bank.**

1. The most valuable invention in my life is my cell phone. _____, my cell phone keeps me connected to my friends and family no matter where I am. Even if someone is in another country, it's easy to make long-distance calls with a cell phone. _____, my cell phone can do lots of other things besides making calls. For instance, I can text messages, browse the Internet, and take pictures. _____, I feel safer with my cell phone. For example, I can use it in an emergency if my car breaks down or I get lost. My cell phone is small in size, but it is a big help to me.

2. Riding a bicycle is a smart way to travel. _____, riding a bike is much cheaper than driving a car because you never have to buy gas. _____, riding a bike is a great way to exercise and stay in shape. _____, riding a bicycle is much better for the environment than driving a car or taking a bus because bikes do not create any pollution. As you can see, there are many advantages to riding a bike, no matter where you live.

WRITING ABOUT YOUR OPINIONS

Prewriting

A. **State your opinion by completing the sentences with *should* or *should not*. Then share your opinions with a partner.**

1. Police officers _____ carry a gun.

2. All students _____ learn a second language.

3. It _____ be illegal for people to use cell phones while they are driving.

4. Animals _____ be used in scientific research.

5. Companies _____ make people retire when they are sixty-five years old.

6. Parents _____ limit the amount of time their children spend on the Internet.

7. Students _____ take a year off between high school and college.

8. Teachers _____ give homework on the weekends.

9. High schools _____ require students to wear uniforms.

10. Colleges and universities _____ offer all courses online.

B. **Choose three of the opinions you wrote in Exercise A and give two or three reasons to support each one.**

A. **Opinion:**

_____

Reason 1:

_____

Reason 2:

_____

Reason 3:

_____

B. Opinion:

_____

Reason 1:

_____

Reason 2:

_____

Reason 3:

_____

C. Opinion:

_____

Reason 1:

_____

Reason 2:

_____

Reason 3:

_____

Writing

Choose one of your opinions as the topic sentence for a paragraph. Then use your reasons to write supporting sentences. Organize your reasons from least important to most important. Remember to use signal words. Give your paragraph a title.

_____

_____

_____

_____

_____

_____

_____

_____

_____

_____

Revising

A. Exchange paragraphs with a partner. Read the paragraph your partner wrote. Then use the Revising Checklist to help your partner improve his or her paragraph.

REVISING CHECKLIST	YES	NO
1. Does the topic sentence state the author's opinion?		
2. Are there at least three reasons to support the opinion?		
3. Are the reasons organized according to order of importance?		
4. Does the paragraph include signal words?		

B. Use your partner's suggestions to revise your paragraph on a separate piece of paper. Put it in your portfolio.

WRITING ABOUT LEARNING ENGLISH

Prewriting

A. Work with a group of three or four students. Make a list of five things people should and should not do when they are learning English. Write complete sentences using *should* or *should not*.

Helpful Hints for Learning English

1. _____
2. _____
3. _____
4. _____
5. _____

B. Compare your list with another group's. Did you have any of the same ideas?

Writing

Write a paragraph giving advice about learning English. Begin with a topic sentence. Use some of the ideas from your list for the supporting sentences. Give at least three reasons for your opinion. Organize your sentences by order of importance and include signal words. End your paragraph with a concluding sentence. Remember to add a title.

_____

_____

_____

_____

_____

_____

_____

_____

_____

_____

Revising

A. Exchange paragraphs with a partner. Read the paragraph your partner wrote. Then use the Revising Checklist to help your partner improve his or her paragraph.

REVISING CHECKLIST	YES	NO
1. Does the topic sentence state the author's opinion?		
2. Are there at least three reasons to support the opinion?		
3. Is there a concluding sentence?		
4. Are the sentences organized according to order of importance?		
5. Does the paragraph include signal words?		

B. Use your partner's suggestions to revise your paragraph on a separate piece of paper. Put it in your portfolio.

Prewriting

A. **Throughout history, people have invented new things to make life better, easier, and safer. Look at the pictures. Write the name of each invention under the correct picture. Use words from the word bank.**

INVENTIONS WORD BANK		
airplane	light bulb	telephone
car	penicillin	telescope
computer	printing press	TV

1. _____   2. _____   3. _____

4. _____   5. _____   6. _____

7. _____   8. _____   9. _____

B. Discuss these questions in small groups.

1. Which three inventions do you think had the biggest effects on society? Why?
2. How do these inventions help people?
3. How do you think these inventions changed the way people live?
4. What other inventions do you think had a big effect on our lives? Make a list.

_____   _____

_____   _____

C. Which invention do you think has had the greatest effect on society? Write your name and opinion in the chart. Ask people in your group. Complete the chart with their opinions.

NAME	MOST IMPORTANT INVENTION

D. Now think of three reasons why you chose the invention. Write your opinion and the three reasons on the lines.

Opinion: _____

Reason 1: _____

Reason 2: _____

Reason 3: _____

Writing

Write a paragraph about the invention you think has had the biggest impact on society. Support your opinion with at least three reasons. Remember to organize your paragraph according to order of importance, and use signal words. Give your paragraph a title.

_____

_____

_____

_____

_____

_____

_____

_____

Revising

A. Exchange paragraphs with a partner. Read the paragraph your partner wrote. Then use the Revising Checklist to help your partner improve his or her paragraph.

REVISING CHECKLIST	YES	NO
1. Does the topic sentence state the author's opinion?		
2. Are there at least three reasons to support the opinion?		
3. Are the sentences organized according to order of importance?		
4. Does the paragraph include signal words?		

B. Use your partner's suggestions to revise your paragraph on a separate piece of paper. Give it the title "The Most Important Invention" and put it in your portfolio.

USE YOUR IMAGINATION

Giving Advice

A. Read the letter to the Adviser. Then read the Adviser's response. Discuss the situation and the response with a partner.

Dear Adviser

Dear Adviser,

Earlier this year, I met a wonderful man named Joel. We fell in love immediately, and we have been dating for about six months now. The problem is that he is still dating other women. I want him to stop seeing other women and date only me. Sometimes I have trouble expressing myself when I am talking to people. I think maybe I should send him an e-mail asking him to stop seeing other women. That way, we wouldn't have to see each other's faces. What do you think I should do?

Thank you,
Confused

Dear Confused,

I think you can and you should talk to Joel face to face. You should not send him an e-mail on such an important subject. A good relationship is based on open communication. You should talk to Joel, forget him, or wait and see how your relationship develops. It is a bad idea to send him an e-mail instead of talking to him directly.

Good luck!

Sincerely,
The Adviser

B. Write your own letter to the Adviser.

Dear Adviser,

_____

_____

_____

_____

_____

_____

_____

_____

_____

_____

C. Exchange letters with a partner. Write a response to your partner's letter.

Dear _____ ,

_____

_____

_____

_____

_____

_____

_____

_____

Sincerely,
The Adviser

D. Read and discuss the responses you and your partner wrote to each other's letters.

ON YOUR OWN

Write a paragraph supporting one of the opinions below. State your opinion in the topic sentence and then support it with several specific reasons or examples. Remember to organize your paragraph according to order of importance, and use signal words. When you are done with your first draft, use the Revising Checklist on page 141 to improve your paragraph.

- Hotels (should or should not) allow pets.
- People turning sixty-five should have to retake the driver's test to keep their license.
- Television commercials have a bad effect on children.
- Single-sex (all-girl or all-boy) schools are a good idea.
- There are several (advantages or disadvantages) of using credit cards.
- Living in the country is better than living in the city. OR Living in the city is better than living in the country.
- Students should be required to spend a certain amount of time doing volunteer work in order to graduate.

YOU BE THE EDITOR

The paragraph below has four mistakes with *should*. With a partner, find and correct the mistakes.

Reading to Young Children

Parents should to read to their young children every day. First of all, reading to young children is important because it is an excellent way to bond with them. In addition, young children whose parents read to them have better language skills when they start school. Parents should spending time talking about the stories and pictures. They shoulds also explain the meanings of new words. Most importantly, these children often develop a love for reading as they grow older. These are only a few of the reasons that parents no should think reading to young children is a waste of time.

Writing a Letter to the Editor

A. **Read the letter to the editor in today's newspaper about teaching art to children.**

LETTERS TO THE EDITOR

Dear Editor:

Last week the Board of Education voted to cut art classes from our schools. The board obviously doesn't understand the importance of art. The board is right in saying that math, science, history, etc., are important for children to learn. It is also right in saying that sports are important for kids' health. The board is wrong, however, to ignore the creative side of children. People need art. Art helps us express ourselves.

Before the members of the school board make a decision about the education of children, they should educate themselves about the importance of art in our lives. The purpose of our schools is to educate. Is a child educated if he or she doesn't know how to draw? The purpose of education is to help children become well-rounded adults. Art is a subject worth studying.

Yours truly,
A Reader

B. **Write a letter to the editor expressing your opinion about teaching art in school. Do you agree with the above letter? Why or why not?**

LETTERS TO THE EDITOR

Dear Editor:

_____

_____

_____

_____

_____

_____

Yours truly,
A Reader

APPENDIX 1

Alphabet and Penmanship

Lowercase and Uppercase Printed Letters

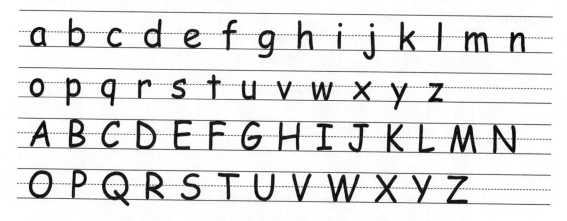

Lowercase and Uppercase Cursive Letters

APPENDIX 2

Past Form of Common Irregular Verbs

Most English verbs are regular. Regular verbs add *-ed* for the past form. English also has many irregular verbs. The following is a list of common irregular verbs and their past forms.

become/became	find/found	meet/met	teach/taught
begin/began	fly/flew	put/put	tell/told
bring/brought	get/got	raise/rose	think/thought
build/built	give/gave	run/ran	understand/
buy/bought	go/went	say/said	understood
come/came	have/had	see/saw	wake/woke
do/did	hear/heard	sell/sold	win/won
drive/drove	hit/hit	sleep/slept	write/wrote
eat/ate	know/knew	speak/spoke	
fall/fell	leave/left	spend/spent	
feel/felt	make/made	take/took	

APPENDIX 3

Punctuation Rules

Punctuation is used to organize written words and guide the reader.

Apostrophe

- Use an apostrophe to show possession.

    My car broke down, so I borrowed Jason's.

- Use an apostrophe to write contractions.

    Yuki isn't going to class today.
    Wally can't find his calculator.
    Why weren't you at the game Saturday?

Comma

- Use a comma to separate three or more words in a list.

    Maria bought apples, oranges, and blueberries at the store.

- Use a comma to separate the day and year in a date.

    They got married on June 29, 2003.

- Use a comma after the name when you write a letter to a friend.

    Dear Henri,

- Use a comma between the name of a city and a state.

    They live in Austin, Texas.

- Use a comma after the words *yes* and *no* in a sentence.

    Yes, I got your message.

- Use a comma when you use *and*, *but*, or *so* to connect two sentences.

    We will visit my grandmother, and we will also see my aunt.
    Keiko went to the library, but it was closed.
    I lost my book, so I didn't do my homework.

- Use a comma when you start a sentence with the words *after*, *although*, *because*, *before*, *if*, *since*, *when*, or *while*.

    Because it was raining, she took an umbrella.
    If he is late again, I will be very angry.
    Since she studies all the time, she is a good student.

- Do not use a comma when the words *after*, *although*, *because*, *before*, *if*, *since*, *when*, or *while* are in the middle of a sentence.

    She took an umbrella although it wasn't raining.
    We waited outside while he talked to the doctor.
    I had something to eat before I went to the movie.

YOU BE THE EDITOR ANSWER KEY

Chapter 1, p. 12

A Lucky and Happy Man

My name is Stanley *S*toico. I am ninety years old. *I* am from *i*taly. I moved to San Diego, *C*alifornia, with my family when I was nine years old. I speak *i*talian and *E*nglish. *i*n my younger years, I had many different jobs. I worked hard and saved my money. In 1965, I started my own business. *T*he business was successful, and *I* i retired in 1993. I like to travel and play golf. I have seen and done a lot in my long life. I am a lucky and happy man.

Chapter 2, p. 25

My Cousin

My cousin's name is Bettina Lee. She is thirty-seven years old. She was born in Chicago, Illinois, but now *she* ~~her~~ lives in Denver, Colorado. She is married and has two children. Bettina and *I* ~~me~~ enjoy spending time together. *We* ~~Us~~ love to go ice-skating. Bettina is an excellent ice-skater. She skated in ice shows when *she* ~~he~~ was young. Now Bettina teaches ice-skating to young children. She enjoys watching *them* ~~their~~.

Chapter 3, p. 40

A Tired New Mother

I am a proud but tired mother of twin baby boys. I don't ~~has~~ *have* any free time these days. My days ~~am~~ *are* very busy, and my nights are busy, too. I never ~~gets~~ *get* much sleep anymore. I wake up several times during the night to feed the babies. They ~~have~~ *are* always hungry! So, I am tired in the morning. I try to take naps when the babies are napping, but I have so much to do. I wash baby clothes and blankets every morning and evening. I also ~~changes~~ *change* diapers all day long. Sometimes when both babies ~~cries~~ *cry* at the same time, I cry, too. But when I ~~watches~~ *watch* them sleeping peacefully, I know how lucky I am to have two happy, healthy babies.

Chapter 4, p. 53

A Delicious Drink

Turkish coffee is not easy to make, but it is delicious. There are several ~~way~~ *ways* to make Turkish coffee, but this is the way my friend taught me. First, you will need a special pot called a *cezve*.  Pour 3 cups of cold ~~waters~~ *water* into the pot. Then, add 3 teaspoons of coffee and 3 teaspoons of ~~sugars~~ *sugar* to the water. Next, heat the water on a low flame until you can see foam forming on top.

Don't let it boil. Then take the pot off the heat. Gently stir the mixture and return it to the heat. Repeat this two more ~~time~~ *times*. Finally, pour the coffee into 3 cups. Make sure each ~~people~~ *person* gets some ~~foams~~ *foam* and enjoy your coffee.

Chapter 5, p. 70

A Busy Pharmacist and Mother

I am a pharmacist and a mother, and my days are busy. As a pharmacist,

my job is to prepare and sell medicines. Every morning, I get up ~~on~~ _at_ 6:30 A.M.

I have breakfast with my family and make lunch for my daughter to take to

school. I leave the house at 8:00 A.M. and drive to the drugstore where I work

~~for~~ _from_ 9:00 A.M. ~~at~~ _to_ 5:00 P.M. During the day, I fill prescriptions for customers.

Sometimes the customers have questions about their medicines. I answer their

questions. I also give them information about how often to take the medicine.

After work, I drive home and have dinner with my family. Then I help my

daughter with her homework ~~during~~ _for_ a few hours. Sometimes I read or watch

TV ~~at~~ _in_ the evening before I go to bed. I am very busy, but I really enjoy being a

pharmacist and a mother.

Chapter 6, p. 91

A Birthday Gift

My brother's birthday is next week, and I want to buy him a ~~news~~ _new_ sweater.

I saw one on the Internet that is made in Canada. I think he will like it. It's a

striped _blue_ sweater. My brother has _blue_ eyes, so it will look nice on him. The

sweater is made of soft wool, so it is ~~warms~~ _warm_. It fits loosely, so it is _comfortable_

to wear. He can wear it to work or on weekends. I'm so happy I had this idea,

and I think my brother will be happy, too!

A Messy Bedroom

My son's bedroom is a mess. He didn't make his bed or hang up his
clothes. There ~~is~~ *are* dirty clothes ~~in~~ *on* the floor. I even found dirty clothes ~~between~~ *under*
his bed. His schoolbooks and papers are all over his desk. There ~~are~~ *is* an empty
soda can ~~of~~ *on* his night table. The top of his dresser is covered with newspapers
and magazines. There ~~are~~ *is* a wet towel on the chair instead of ~~at~~ *in* the laundry
basket. I wish he would clean up his room!

My First Camping Trip

My first camping trip was not at all what I expected. My brother and I
packed our car Friday afternoon and ~~drived~~ *drove* five hours to a beautiful campsite
in Maine. I ~~thinked~~ *thought* it would be hard to put up our tent, but it ~~were~~ *was* easy. It only
took a few minutes. We made a fire and cooked a delicious dinner over the
fire. We ~~enjoy~~ *enjoyed* a beautiful sunset. Then we went into the tent and ~~falled~~ *fell* asleep
surrounded by the peace and quiet of the trees. There were no bugs and no
bears. It rained a little in the night, but we were warm and dry in our tent.
When we ~~woked~~ *woke* up, the sun was out and we took a walk along the river.
What a surprise. I like camping!

Reading to Young Children

Parents should ~~to~~ read to their young children every day. First of all, reading to young children is important because it is an excellent way to bond with them. In addition, young children whose parents read to them have better language skills when they start school. Parents should ~~spending~~ *spend* time talking about the stories and pictures. They ~~shoulds~~ *should* also explain the meanings of new words. Most importantly, these children often develop a love for reading as they grow older. These are only a few of the reasons that parents ~~no~~ should *not* think reading to young children is a waste of time.